YOUR4 DISCIPLESHIP

By Brett Bodiford

Fostering Motivation & Spiritual Engagement

"These that have turned

the world upside down

are come hither also"

Acts 17:6b

ISBN 978-1-7347089-0-5

Published by YOUR4 Ministries
238 Lake Drive
Barnwell Sc 29812

Edited by Cup and Quill Editing and Publication Services, LLC

Foreword by Jake Edwards, Senior Pastor Crossroads Aiken, SC

DEDICATION

To my wife Becky who deserves the credit. This Preacher is only successful because of the woman God gave me. She is a gift from God, and He knows what He is doing.

CONTENTS

CONTENTS

FOREWORD

Throughout my childhood, I frequently recall my family hurriedly, sometimes even frantically, getting ready for Sunday morning church. On these mornings each week, the worries and stresses of life suddenly disappeared once we left home. It was as though our fears and anxieties knew that when we went to church they had to stay home. For two whole hours, we were a family unit that would rival the happiest and most well-organized families around. On this day, our family struggles were certainly not forgotten but assuredly not discussed until we again greeted life's hardships at the threshold of our home. They were all unforgivably ready to mount themselves upon our shoulders the very moment we walked through the door. It seemed they were waiting on us, watching for us to come down the road and near the house. I could feel the tension begin to rise once we pulled in the driveway. It was time to pick-up the baggage we had, earlier that morning, checked at the door. This was a heavy burden for our family. We often felt exhausted, isolated, frustrated, and overwhelmed - teetering on the edge of giving up.

While we can never escape life's difficulties, yet if we keep in mind that struggling alone in these circumstances is not God's design for us or our families? What if we remembered that God created a support network of strength among those around us for our journey with Him in this life? We do not have to feel exhausted, alone, frustrated, and overwhelmed, teetering on the edge of giving up. On the contrary, we are doing life with those around us and depending on God, as He intended. Our difficult circumstances will be outmatched by the support network God has given or will provide if we are willing to live in the Biblical community with other believers.

I have been serving in ministry since 2000 and have had the exciting opportunity to plant Crossroads Church in Aiken, SC. Over the years of my ministry, I have come to recognize that most Christians often struggle to individually remain obedient to God's command to make disciples. The last words of Jesus in Matthew 28:19-20 are a mandate and priority for every believer. The moment before Jesus ascends into heaven, he takes a moment to share one last encouragement, and this is what Jesus says, *"Go therefore and make disciples of all nations, baptizing them in the name of the Father and of the Son and of the Holy Spirit, teaching them to observe all that I have commanded you. And behold, I am with you always, to the end of the age."* This was not intended to be a practice of the institution of the church alone; it was a call to individuals to make disciples of others in all nations, beginning with our own. If we are not individually making disciples, we are not living "on" or "for" God's missional mandate. Instead, we are living a "mission" of our own governance based on our fleshly agenda and personal comforts and perspectives. When we depend on the institution of the church and fail to be individuals who disciple one another, we give in to a false sense of what Discipleship is. This leads to struggling individuals and families feeling exhausted, isolated, frustrated, and overwhelmed, teetering on the edge of giving up.

I have been in many discussions with people over the years centered around the topic of Discipleship. Often, the following question is posed: "If we were responsible for the spiritual development of another, what would we do?" Frequently, people respond, "To be honest, I don't know how to disciple someone." We must all come to grips with the fact the Bible requires each follower of Jesus to be responsible for the spiritual development of another. We see in this book that scripture makes this unmistakably clear and should not be ignored or overlooked. We cannot merely skim an entire passage and pick out what we like while disregarding what does not fit our current self-made plans and comforts. Discipleship is more than pointing someone to an institution, event, or program. Biblical Discipleship requires us to journey alongside one-another - encouraging, caring, and challenging each other in personal and spiritual development. Your4 Discipleship will guide us step by step through a technique which will place us right in the heart of Discipleship.

As I tell my wife, Jennifer, "my YOUR4 group night is one of my favorite nights of the week". I become refreshed and feel supported and encouraged. As well, there is nothing more exciting than to see my YOUR4 group find profound truths in God's Word and commit to personal life change among one another. This offers other group members the opportunity to encourage, pray for, and connect with one another as they make life changes. People need to know they are not alone in life's difficulties and struggles. We are called to bear each other's burdens, which helps prevent feeling exhausted, isolated, frustrated, and overwhelmed. Discipleship encourages people to not throw in the towel and give up!

YOUR4 is a guide that will help keep people fixed firmly on God's word as well as engaged in a discussion on the intended meanings in scripture, which lead to Discipleship and spiritual development. As I have made YOUR4 Discipleship a consistent method of choice in my journey to become a disciple-maker, my life is and will continue to be enriched both personally and spiritually.

Jake Edwards

Senior Pastor Crossroads Church Aiken

ACKNOWLEDGMENTS

This work would not be possible without the encouragement and support of the people Christ placed in my life. My wife and children Becky, Joshua (Reigh), Nicklaus (Jade), and Jenna (who currently resides with the Lord). My mama who always encouraged and supported me in following God's call regardless of this world's view.

Pastor Jake Edwards for his encouragement and support. A Pastor yes but mostly a part of the body of Christ and my brother. Thank you for your unwavering support and kick in the pants.

INTRODUCTION

Journeying through YOUR4 Discipleship will be a rewarding experience as we learn to walk closer with Christ and follow His guidance. Today, adversity may cripple us emotionally and spiritually. Adversity in our life will increase as we discover God's plan for our lives and begin to converge with Him and triverge with others. Triverge means bringing others into our walk with Christ, thereby creating accountability and a support system that will help us through adversity. Genesis 50:20 gives us an indication of how adversity should be seen by Christians.

> **20** *But as for you, ye thought evil against me; but God meant it unto good, to bring to pass, as it is this day, to save much people alive.*
>
> *Genesis 50:20*

Our difficulties and responses to them can be a springboard for our testimony and its impact near and far.

YOUR4 Discipleship is laid out with a hiker and climber in mind. This concept is that Christians will learn to move from the simple act of walking to climbing cliffs as they struggle to find finger holds needed to ascend to the next level. Our senses will adjust to see life through the lens of Christ as we seek His will in our lives.

Hikers determine the difficulty of a hike based on a class numbering system. This system typically covers classes 1-5, with one being a path and five being rock climbing. Below are the classes based on where we are in our hiking and climbing adventure with Christ.

Class 1 hiking or the very first step in convergence will take us through week six. The class 1 hiking trails are those that are low risk. Each step of our class 1 journey is well marked and covers salvation, Baptism, bible study, prayer, community, and sharing Jesus. Class 1 trails will gain some elevation but require no special gear such as climbing ropes or maps. During this first step, we should establish who we are in Christ and where we stand. The views from here will be breathtaking.

Class 2 or week seven requires map reading skills through Bible study and prayerfully thought out responses to God's call. As we seek to continue our climb, it is necessary to steady ourselves as the cliffs of this world try to influence our outcomes. Also, parts of this trail are not marked. These are the areas where we will need to grab our map (Bible) and seek guidance as we proceed. This type of trail can cause unsteadiness due to the loose stones and rocks we must traverse.

Mt. Trivergence is the next challenge staring us down. Through convergence, we learned to become one with God. We trusted Him to lead our life and withheld nothing from Him. Trivergence expands this relationship to include others as we seek to be a called-out disciple of Christ.

Approaching Mt Trivergence, we quickly note that class 3 hiking requires added skills. Like using our hands to grab hold of rocks and crevices pulling ourselves along steep slopes and unprotected terrain. Do not be alarmed as Christ is always there to catch us. The purpose of convergence was to ensure we truly trusted Christ before proceeding into the extreme terrain. Trivergence takes us into the next level of communion, community, and commission. After summitting Mt. Trivergence, we meet back at base camp to discuss the journey. What did it all mean and how did we benefit? Section 2 climbing will provide the background and methods for all we have learned. From here we will launch out as a guide for others.

Triverge bringing others into our walk with Christ, thereby creating accountability and a support system that will help us through adversity.

PART 1

YOUR4 DISCIPLESHIP HIKING

1 WHY YOUR4

The Your4 Discipleship journey will encourage and challenge new and seasoned Christians. Traveling the path to Discipleship will be a memorable and rewarding experience. Learning to question our hearts and prioritize our time will result in spiritual fruit not seen since the Garden of Eden, not including the apple, of course. The next twelve weeks will clarify who we are in Christ. As we seek to understand our desires amid God's will. This clarity will enhance our Christian walk and facilitate our ability to turn the world upside down like the early Christians in Acts.

These that have turned the world upside down are come hither also; (Acts 17:6b)

Throughout YOUR4 Discipleship, we will review the foundation of our current journey as a Christian. Our hiking journey will challenge us to penetrate our heart's hardened outer shell and dig to the core of who we are and what we truly desire. Our calling and real foundational underpinning will be revealed as we see our desires poised against the backdrop of Christ. If we determine our foundational underpinning is based on this world's calling, I beg you to immediately stop and build a salvation relationship with the Father. Never will there be anything in this world more important than a personal relationship with Christ. Gaining an understanding of where we stand foundationally is the only way we can repair or launch our Christian relationship with the Father. In this searching, we will come to realize there are only two choices of foundations, sand, or rock. Matthew 7:24-27 puts it this way:

> *24 Therefore whosoever heareth these sayings of mine and doeth them, I will liken him unto a wise man, which built his house upon a rock:*
>
> *25 And the rain descended, and the floods came, and the winds blew, and beat upon that house; and it fell not: for it was founded upon a rock.*
>
> *26 And everyone that heareth these sayings of mine, and doeth them not, shall be likened unto a foolish man, which built his house upon the sand:*
>
> *27 And the rain descended, and the floods came, and the winds blew, and beat upon that house, and it fell: and great was the fall of it.   Matthew 7:24-27*

Reaching in to seek and expose who we are in Christ exposes our basest desires. We will be forced to wrestle with our heart's desires and the mask we wear like a thief that sneaks around in the dark. Yet this work will pay dividends. The wrestling matches with God's will give us a real unadulterated understanding of ourselves, our calling, and the next steps. Understanding our foundation, we gain the knowledge of our position in Christ; Is God a spectator or decision-maker in our daily walk.

The secondary advantage of giving God total access is understanding our responses to every situation. These responses can be filled with peace and love or anger and dizzying anxiety. Our foundational underpinning will determine our response to life's events. This information is useful to help us understand ourselves and how to help others during difficult circumstances.

Throughout the battles of YOUR4, we will question the depth of our roots and what kind of ground they are growing. We will cultivate an open and honest relationship with God that will ignite a fire this world cannot quench.

YOUR4 Discipleship is designed to equip Christians mentally and emotionally with a backpack overflowing with tools for ministry expansion. This backpack, along with our hiking and climbing adventures, will prepare us for a life of boldly spreading the gospel. Our bold witness of Jesus will become a part of who we are at the core. Spectating will no longer be enough. With our Christian heart fully developed, we will long for service. YOUR4 Discipleship ultimately creates disciples that create disciples.

WHAT IS A DISCIPLE

"Follow me, and I will make you fishers of men."
Matthew 4:19

Disciples are Christ-followers who desire to follow the example set by Christ in His earthly ministry. Fulfilling this desire is the only path for Christians to satisfy the heart, mind, and soul. Christ-followers not only desire to follow Christ's example, but seek to live out this example by seeking the least, the last, and the lost. This longing creates a discipline that leads to a regular life rhythm of the 3Cs: communion, community, and commission. Becoming a disciple calls us back to Matthew 28, where the word "Go" takes on a new meaning as we seek Christ and His personal calling to each of us.

19" Go therefore and make disciples of all nations, baptizing them in the name of the Father and of the Son and the Holy Spirit, 20 teaching them to observe all that I have commanded you. And behold, I am with you always, to the end of the age." Matthew 28:19-20

Not only will the disciple live by Christ's example and "Go." They will also submit all of who they are and what they have for God's glory.

"But seek ye first the kingdom of God, and his righteousness;" Matthew 6:33

Seeking Christ's kingdom and righteousness creates a love for others. In the face of hate, persecution, and bitterness, the disciple seeks to repay with kindness. This display of love will glorify God and generate questions from those that do not know the truth. This type of love sees the world as a mission field that must be harvested.

WHO BENEFITS FROM YOUR4?

The YOUR4 Discipleship will benefit newborn Christians to senior Pastors. Both seek the truth of Christ. Whether for themselves or those who do not know the truth.

> *9 And Jesus said unto him, this day is salvation come to this house, forsomuch as he also is a son of Abraham. 10 For the Son of man is come to seek and to save that which was lost.*
>
> *Luke 19:9-10*

YOUR4 is for the young Christian who is unsure of what to do next. YOUR4 Discipleship takes us from the basics of what to do after salvation through reaching our community and, ultimately, the world.

The seasoned Christian up to the senior pastor can benefit by following YOUR4 and engaging the people God has entrusted to our care. Through YOUR4, we can create groups with the understanding that Christians are called to be relational and supportive with other Christians while reaching out to those that do not know the truth of God's grace. As both groups seek God's guidance, each will ultimately come to understand how God loves, who God is, and what God's eternal grace contains. The body is called to Christ, to one another, and to those we meet throughout our daily lives.

Our foundational

underpinning will

determine our response

to life's events.

CONVERGENCE

 YOUR4 Discipleship

2 THE WHAT'S WE ASK

<u>What's in It for Me?</u>

Biblically Correct Walk

Closer Relationships

Heart for the Broken

Life Change

Community

<u>What's… Required?</u>

Daily S.O.A.P.

Daily Prayer

Bi-weekly group meeting

Open discussions

Actions to Grow & Develop Spiritually

<u>What's…needed?</u>

Learn to S.O.A.P.

There are several methods of learning God's Word. The S.O.A.P. method allows the reader time to recognize what the scripture says.

How do I S.O.A.P.?

<u>Scripture</u>: Read the verse or verses in the weekly S.O.A.P. scripture each day several times slowly. Notice each word and its placement.

<u>Observation:</u> Track our observations about the passage. Do we notice any words that stand out and lead to a guiding principle?

<u>Application:</u> Consider if we can apply the scripture to our everyday life. Consider how to do it in your daily walk.

<u>Prayer:</u> Write a personal prayer based on our observations and applications.

PRIORITY CIRCLE 1

Priority circles and time studies allow us to take a fresh, unbiased look into our hearts regarding our relationship with God. Often, we evaluate our relationship with Christ by seeking justification of our wants and desires and never genuinely searching for God's calling. This type of evaluation is self-serving and destructive to our victorious Christian relationship. Understanding how we stack the deck in our favor should create within the disciple a need to have an honest evaluation before Christ. Such an assessment ought to deal only in facts, deny the self, and glorify the Father. Priority circles and time studies should become a regular part of our walk as a disciple.

The priority circle is an unbiased personal look at where Christ stands in our lives. This is not a test but rather a peek into our heart where the real man resides. The Christian walk must start with a thorough understanding of the heart.

¹⁹ As in water face answereth to face, so the heart of man to man. Proverbs 27:19

Do not fill in what you think is correct. Fill in how you currently see life. The center is the top priority. From there, work outwards. Objectively evaluate time, money, and emotional capital.

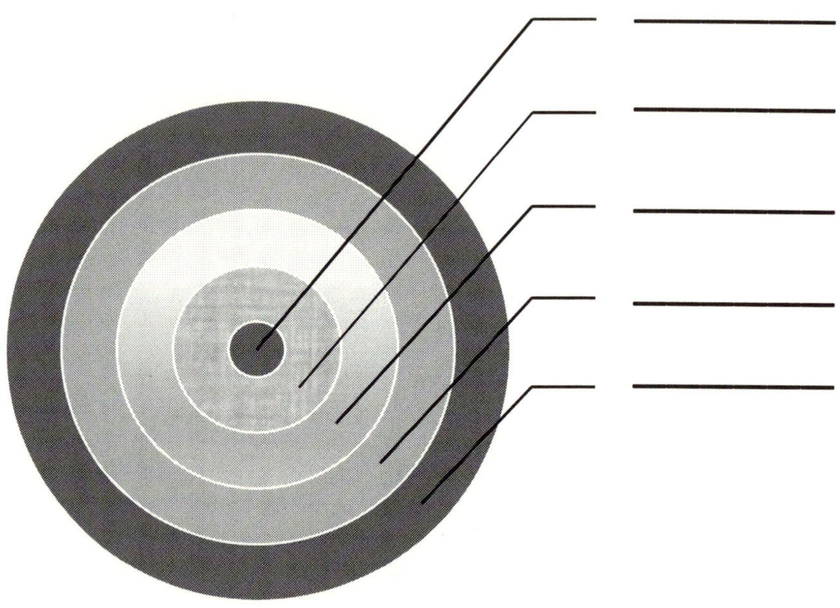

TIME STUDY – 1

Evaluating how we prioritize time will direct us toward crushing the claim that we "don't have time." Track your day in round numbers, say from six in the morning until eleven at night. Identify where and how you spend your time. This study must be an honest evaluation between God and us.

Example: Up at 6; Work from 7-4; Cook 5-6; TV 6-10; Ready for Bed 11

The study can be simple if you are like me, and most of your days adhere to a routine. The time study will indicate the items that you have determined are most important. Complete the chart below for an average day.

TASK TITLE	Time Hours

Stepping Into YOUR4 Discipleship

Throughout YOUR4 Discipleship, the steps remain straight forward and consistent. These include individual missions, relationship building, relational and missional community, and coaching. Below is a simple outline of each step.

Weekly actions allow engagement with God through His Word and help us share our walk with others in YOUR4 group. This sharing may involve any number of methods: text, calls, lunch, coffee, or Zoom. The goal is to build relationships with one another, allowing the community to form, and reflect the light of Christ to the world. This light not only streams outward to the world but will reach into the life of each member as trust is built through investment.

S.O.A.P. - Scripture, Observation, Application, and Prayer. S.O.A.P. is the method described above used to evaluate verses each day as we learn to invest our time with God. As we S.O.A.P. each verse, one main topic should develop, creating a six-word hiking trail by week's end. This hiking trail points us toward God and His calling.

YOUR4 Their Journey – As early as possible, start praying that God will reveal four people in our life to become a YOUR4 group with you as a leader. In week six, you will list the four people you are praying for and contact each one through texts, calls, coffee, or other means of communication. Establishing connections initiates commission and allows us to participate in the calling of God to "Go ye therefore."

Priority Circle & Time Analysis – We will complete three separate priority circles and time analyses during the twelve weeks of YOUR4 Hiking. Throughout, YOUR4 priority circles and time studies take place immediately before starting the first week of S.O.A.P, after the completion of week eight, and upon completion of our twelve-week program.

Priority circles and time studies are to evaluate ourselves, considering who God is in our life. We may share them if you like, but we do not have to. Acknowledging the need for honesty between God and ourselves allows us to look within while also looking up and out for guidance. Understanding our hearts will help us as we endeavor to draw closer to God through self-evaluation. Remember to pray and read God's Word daily, as we complete these essential evaluations. Use these guidelines as a grading system. It will equip us to see our paths with clear eyes and open hearts, removing bias and preconceived notions of our Christian life. Do not worry about what we discover as we go through the processes; God is already aware of what we will find. Christ wants us to be truthful with Him and to desire His presence in our lives.

<u>Coffee Talk</u> – This program offers time to live in a relational community. Typically, we will bring one S.O.A.P. from the previous two weeks. These S.O.A.P.S are conversation starters and allow us to answer questions together. Additionally, we delve deeper into the Word. Coffee talk can become organic, thereby developing a Christian life together. Learning to live life together creates relational ministry within the group, which is integral to developing the body of Christ. This type of ministry calls our hearts into living life as Christ desires in the book of Mark.

31 And the second is like, namely this, thou shalt love thy neighbor as thyself. There is none other commandment greater than these. Mark 12:31

Scheduling coffee talk ahead of time is not required, but we strongly encourage this type of preplanning. Participants in YOUR4 should make every effort to attend each coffee talk. Nothing can substitute for the time spent together with fellow Christians as we learn to place God and His work at the forefront of our life. Coffee talks are where we learn to trust one another and build relationships that allow more open dialogue.

Coffee Talk Schedule:

Week	Location	Date
Week 2		
Week 4		
Week 6		
Week 8		
Week 10		
Week 12		

<u>Miscellaneous.</u> - There will be multiple types of miscellaneous items throughout YOUR4. These are designed to challenge and expose where we are in our walk with Christ and our devotion to loving others.

Another miscellaneous item is text messages. This is one area that does not need to be overthought as we learn to communicate with others about our faith. It is as simple as sending, "I just prayed for you. What are your plans for today? What application did you get from today's verse? I think ___ about today's verse, how about you?" Texting and calling do not have to be complicated. We are learning to be comfortable when we reach out to others and train ourselves to think of others during our devotion time.

Nothing can be substituted for the time spent together with fellow Christians as we learn to place God and His work at the forefront of our life.

 YOUR4 Discipleship

WEEK 1 SALVATION

The Twentieth Century Dictionary describes salvation as follows:

<u>Salvation</u>: 1. The act of saving: preservation from destruction, danger, and great calamity. 2. In theology, the redemption of man from the bondage of sin and liability to eternal death and conferring on him everlasting happiness. [1]

The above definition of salvation describes one part of what God has completed on our behalf. God has given us something that extends into the past, currently resides in the present, and proceeds us into the future. The sudden release from the bondage of sin upon salvation begs the question: What now? How do we move forward within the grace that has been bestowed on our past, present, and future? Starting this week, we begin to answer that very question as we strike out on our hiking trail seeking answers to these questions. Traveling each hiking trail of Discipleship quickly moves us from self-focus to relational community. No longer are we satisfied living an independent life of self-service. Our desires begin to align with those of Jesus. The desire to live in a missional community with each other is brought to life. This week's hiking adventure delves into salvation as we discover the next steps along the way.

---

[1] Twentieth Century Dictionary, 1939

 YOUR4 Discipleship

Weekly Actions

- S.O.A.P. verses 1-6 relating to salvation
  - Text one person from the YOUR4 group (scripture, encouragement, etc.).

Weekly Scripture

1. John 3:16
2. Philippians 2:12
3. Matthew 22:39
4. Deuteronomy 8:6
5. Matthew 16:24

Matthew 7:13-14

Week 1: Monday	Salvation
Scripture: John 3:16 Date:	
Observation:	
Application:	
Prayer:	

 YOUR4 Discipleship

Week 1: Tuesday	Salvation

Scripture: Philippians 2:12   Date:

Observation:

Application:

Prayer:

Week 1: Wednesday	Salvation

Scripture: Matthew 22:39   Date:

Observation:

Application:

Prayer:

Week 1: Thursday	Salvation

Scripture: Deuteronomy 8:6   Date:

Observation:

Application:

Prayer:

Week 1: Friday	Salvation

Scripture: Matthew 16:24   Date:

Observation:

Application:

Prayer:

Week 1: Saturday	Salvation

Scripture: Matthew 7:13-14   Date:

Observation:

Application:

Prayer:

Week 1: Who I texted? Why?

Name:

⁹ Who hath saved us, and called us with an holy calling, not according to our works, but according to his own purpose and grace, which was given us in Christ Jesus before the world began,

2 Timothy 1:9

WEEK 2: BAPTISM BOLD FAITH

Baptism is our public declaration of faith and the first step after salvation as we turn our life over to Christ. Obedience to step one opens the door for steps two through infinity. The relational community that supports us in Baptism will be invaluable as we face life's tough challenges following God. Lean into who Christ is with one another while seeking to live a Godly life. Our hiking adventure takes us to the water this week as we dive into Baptism and stir the waters of our soul.

And as the circumcised in the flesh, and not in the heart, have no part in God's good promises; even so they that be baptized in the flesh, and not in heart, have no part in Christ's blood.

– William Tyndale

Weekly Actions

- S.O.A.P. verses below concerning Baptism
- Text one person from the YOUR4 group (scripture, encouragement, etc.)
- Engage in Coffee Talk with YOUR4 group. Bring one S.O.A.P. from week 1 or 2

Weekly Scripture

1. Matthew 10:32-33
2. Matthew 3:13-17
3. Acts 2:37-38
4. Acts 2:41
5. Acts 2:47

John 14:21

Week 2: Monday	Baptism Bold Faith

Scripture: Matthew 20:32-33   Date:

Observation:

Application:

Prayer:

| Week 2: Tuesday | Baptism Bold Faith |

Scripture: Matthew 3:13-17   Date:

Observation:

Application:

Prayer:

Week 2: Wednesday	Baptism Bold Faith

Scripture: Acts 2:37-38   Date:

Observation:

Application:

Prayer:

| Week 2: Thursday | Baptism Bold Faith |

Scripture: Acts 2:41   Date:

Observation:

Application:

Prayer:

Week 2: Friday	Baptism Bold Faith

Scripture: Acts 2:47   Date:

Observation:

Application:

Prayer:

 YOUR4 Discipleship

Week 2: Saturday	Baptism Bold Faith

Scripture: John 14:21   Date:

Observation:

Application:

Prayer:

Person I Texted?

S.O.A.P. I am taking to Coffee Talk?

Soap Week #:

Verse:

What speaks personally to me about this S.O.A.P.? How do I apply this daily?

YOUR4 Discipleship

WEEK 3: BIBLICALLY INFLUENCED LIFE
COMMUNION WITH GOD

No other book on earth has answers to every conundrum man faces. The Bible is life's instruction manual. Without a faithful study of the Word, we will always act from our vantage point instead of learning and understanding the correct biblical action or reaction to life's circumstances. Learning to lean into the Bible and apply the directions freely given, draws us close to God publicly and privately. As we continue to learn God's way, our paths will be directed in a way that peace will prevail in every troublesome situation. This week we slow our hiking adventure and sit by the campfire with the Word of God.

10 Be still and know that I am God: I will be exalted among the heathen, I will be exalted in the earth.

Psalm 46:10

Weekly Actions

- S.O.A.P. verses below concerning Bible study
- Text one person from the YOUR4 group (scripture, encouragement, etc.)

Weekly Scripture

1. Hebrews 4:12
2. 2 Timothy 3:16-17
3. Matthew 28:18-20
4. Psalm 119:9
5. Psalm 119:182
6. 2 Timothy 2:15

Week 3: Monday	Bible Influenced Life

Scripture: Hebrews 4:12   Date:

Observation:

Application:

Prayer:

Week 3: Tuesday	Bible Influenced Life

Scripture: 2 Timothy 3:16-17 Date:

Observation:

Application:

Prayer:

Week 3: Wednesday	Bible Influenced Life

Scripture: Matthew 28:19-20   Date:

Observation:

Application:

Prayer:

Week 3: Thursday	Bible Influenced Life

Scripture: Psalm 119:9   Date:

Observation:

Application:

Prayer:

Week 3: Friday	Bible Influenced Life
Scripture: Psalm 119:82 Date:	
Observation:	
Application:	
Prayer:	

Week 3: Saturday	Bible Influenced Life

Scripture: 2 Timothy 2:15   Date:

Observation:

Application:

Prayer:

Person I texted? Why?

50

WEEK 4: PRAYER GOD & YOU

Prayer: The act or practice of praying to or supplicating the Divine Being; the offering to God of adoration, confession, supplication, and thanksgiving; communion with God in devotional exercises. [2]

Prayer, at times, seems to be an inactive activity. We feel like we should do something tangible while we busily run about. On the contrary, prayer is time communing with God. Our alone time with God is one of the most intimate activities we have as Christians. Time separated from the world in direct conversation with God is powerful. This power is not only displayed in our lives but in

> *"To be a Christian without prayer is no more possible than to be alive without breathing."* Martin Luther

---

[2] Twentieth Century Dictionary, 1939

the lives of those for whom we pray. The act of prayer will create within each Christian a tender mind and heart, ultimately drawing us closer to God.

Sometimes that quiet moment speaks volumes to a wounded and broken heart in ways that no man ever could. This week's actions move away from the campfire for a bit. Find some alone time and wander through the woods in prayer and communion with God.

Weekly Actions

- S.O.A.P. verses below concerning prayer
- Call one person from the YOUR4 group (We can ask how they are doing, ask for a prayer request, etc.)
- Coffee Talk with YOUR4. Bring one S.O.A.P. from weeks 3 or 4.
- Fill in How Can I Help section

Weekly Scripture

1. 1 Chronicles 28:9
2. Jeremiah 24:7
3. Mark 1:35
4. Luke 18:1
5. 1 Thessalonians 5:17
6. 1 Corinthians 10:13

Week 4: Monday	Prayer God & You

Scripture: 1 Chronicles 28:9   Date:

Observation:

Application:

Prayer:

Week 4: Tuesday	Prayer God & You

Scripture: Jeremiah 24:7   Date:

Observation:

Application:

Prayer:

Week 4: Wednesday	Prayer God & You

Scripture: Mark 1:35   Date:

Observation:

Application:

Prayer:

Week 4: Thursday	Prayer God & You

Scripture: Luke 18:1   Date:

Observation:

Application:

Prayer:

Week 4: Friday	Prayer God & You

Scripture: 1 Thessalonians 5:17   Date:

Observation:

Application:

Prayer:

Week 4: Saturday	Prayer God & You

Scripture: 1 Corinthians 10:13   Date:

Observation:

Application:

Prayer:

Who did I call?

S.O.A.P. Card I am taking to Coffee Talk.

Verse Week:

Verse:

What speaks personally to me about this card?

TELL ME HOW

Your4 is designed to create a relational community that relies on one other.

- As we Hike into week 5, what has been hindering our growth through YOUR4?
- How can your YOUR4 leader give additional support?
- How do you need empowering to enable continuing growth throughout your journey?
- Sharing these hindrances with the group or your leader enables the body of Christ to carry shared burdens.

WEEK 5 LIFE TOGETHER CAMPING
COMMUNITY WITH OTHERS

This week we explore Life Together and the importance of building a biblically based relational community. Learning to be faithful to God's calling is at the core of building long-lasting relational ministry versus connecting for coffee. We often ask God to use us, yet we continually make ourselves unavailable. Such actions are attempts to force God to work within our timetable. We try to squeeze God into a small space on our calendar based on our priorities. As disciples, God and His work must move to the pinnacle of our lives. Moving God to the top of the list places everything else in life in the correct order. This realignment of priorities frees us to create space for ministry and life together. By putting God and his work first, we see God at work in all things and can live victoriously. The Kingdom does not call us to handle life's situations alone. Christ calls us to be a body of one sharing burdens and victories. Let us stop off at the lodge and spend fellowship time together building community.

Weekly Actions

- S.O.A.P. verses below concerning Life Together
- Call one person from YOUR4 group (We can ask how they are doing, or ask for a prayer request, and so on).

Weekly Scripture

1. Romans 12:4-5
2. 1 Corinthians 1:10
3. Ephesians 4:12-14
4. Hebrews 10:24-25
5. Romans 15:14-15
6. 1 Thessalonians 4:18

Week 5: Monday	Life Together Camping

Scripture: Romans 12:4-5   Date:

Observation:

Application:

Prayer:

Week 5: Tuesday	Life Together Camping

Scripture: 1 Corinthians 1:10   Date:

Observation:

Application:

Prayer:

Week 5: Wednesday	Life Together Camping

Scripture: Ephesians 4:12-14   Date:

Observation:

Application:

Prayer:

Week 5: Thursday	Life Together Camping

Scripture: Hebrews 10:24-25   Date:

Observation:

Application:

Prayer:

Week 5: Friday	Life Together Camping

Scripture: Romans 15:14-15   Date:

Observation:

Application:

Prayer:

Week 5: Saturday	Life Together Camping

Scripture: 1 Thessalonians 4:18   Date:

Observation:

Application:

Prayer:

Week 5: Who I called? Why?

WEEK 6: SHARING JESUS
COMMISSION TO THE CULTURE

The life-changing news we have experienced thus far is not for us alone. It must be shared. There is not one person that we get to write off. Christ did not live and die to save some, He died to give grace to all. Even those that we fail to agree with or that have mistreated us. Failing to accept every individual reflects our lack of growth in Christ.

While at the camping lodge, we should be excited to share the good news of Jesus with every man, woman, and child.

<u>Weekly Actions</u>

- S.O.A.P. verses below concerning Sharing Jesus
- Coffee Talk with Group – Come prepared to discuss the four you have chosen to invest your life into.
- <u>Fill in your YOUR4-Their Journey</u>
- Call or text one person from your <u>Your4</u>-Their Journey (scripture, encouragement, etc.)

TELL US WHO? REVEAL YOUR4 AT COFFEE TALK TELL US WHO

With whom will you start your journey?

With whom do you communicate regularly?

With whom do you have a relationship?

This week is a real turning point in YOUR4 Hiking as we invest in others as our leader has invested in us. In the second half of this journey, we seek to build up relational equity with the four people we have chosen. As Christians, we must come to understand that people do not care how much we know until they know how much we care. The following is a list of starter ideas. Of course, it is not inclusive of all the ways to reach out.

List YOUR4 and start building our missional community. Supporting them through prayer, listening, encouragement, discipleship, gifts, text, coffee, and calls. The next page has a potential schedule for you to follow ensuring you are consistent/faithful to the calling of others.

YOUR - YOUR4 – <u>Their Journey Begins Now</u>

Name	**Contact Information**	**Text/Call Schedule**
		Week 6 & 10
		Week 7 & 11
		Week 8 & 12
		Week 9 & 12

1. <u>Weekly Scripture</u>2 Corinthians 4:5-6
2. Ephesians 2:4-5
3. 2 Corinthians 5:18-20
4. 1 John 1:4
5. Romans 10:9
6. Romans 6:2

---

*"The beauty of the world lies
in the diversity of its people."*

Unknown 

Week 6: Monday	Sharing Jesus

Scripture: 2 Corinthians 4:5-6 Date:

Observation:

Application:

Prayer:

Week 6: Tuesday	Sharing Jesus

Scripture: Ephesians 2:4-5 Date:

Observation:

Application:

Prayer:

 YOUR4 Discipleship

Week 6: Wednesday	Sharing Jesus

Scripture: 2 Corinthians 5:18-20 Date:

Observation:

Application:

Prayer:

Week 6: Thursday	Sharing Jesus

Scripture1 John 1:4   Date:

Observation:

Application:

Prayer:

Week 6: Friday	Sharing Jesus

Scripture Romans 10:9   Date:

Observation:

Application:

Prayer:

Week 6: Saturday	Sharing Jesus

Scripture: Romans 6:2 Date:

Observation:

Application:

Prayer:

Who was your YOUR4 Person texted?

What was the reaction from the new potential YOUR4 candidate?

WEEK 7: TRUSTING JESUS
MY JOURNEY - LIFE APPLICATION

How do we maneuver from the act of trusting Christ through prayer and study at home to trusting Him in everyday life? This week will be challenging as the question is posed: Do we trust God with everything?

During the next week, we must be in prayer about how to approach God with our future. This prayer is about seeking His direction for our life. He allows us to decide to follow or not. The narrow or wide gate? (Matthew 7:13-14). It is our decision.

As we approach the peak of Mount Convergence, the gate to the next trail narrows. This is where some decide they will not go any further. As we consider what truly serving Christ, is we must weigh the cost. What is it that we currently will not give to Christ? Is withholding worth the impact it will have on ours and others eternity?

28" For which of you, intending to build a tower, sitteth not down first, and counteth the cost, whether he have sufficient to finish it? 29 Lest haply, after he hath laid the foundation, and is not able to finish it, all that behold it begin to mock him,30Saying, this man began to build and was not able to finish.31 Or what king, going to make war against another king, sitteth not down first, and consulteth whether he be able with ten thousand to meet him that cometh against him with twenty thousand?32 Or else, while the other is yet a great way off, he sendeth an ambassage, and desireth conditions of peace.33 So likewise, whosoever he be of you that forsaketh not all that he hath, he cannot be my disciple.34 Salt is good: but if the salt have lost his savour, wherewith shall it be seasoned?35 It is neither fit for the land nor yet for the dunghill, but men cast it out. He that hath ears to hear let him hear." Luke 14:28-35

There is no option to partially serve. Either Christ is our King or not. There is no middle ground. Christ has called His children to be about His business. We are not of this world. We are sojourners and exiles (1 Peter 2:11), and as followers of Christ will lay our treasures in Heaven. Verse 33 above is self-explanatory. We must give everything to Christ.

Weekly Actions

- S.O.A.P. verses concerning <u>Trusting Jesus</u>
- Call or text one from <u>Your4</u>-Their Journey (scripture, encouragement, etc.)

Weekly Scripture

Time (Ephesians 5:15-16) Set aside time for God

Talent (Colossians 3:17) Seek what you can do for God

Testimony (1 Corinthians 6:19-20) Be bold in your testimony

Treasure (1 Corinthians 16:2) Start tithing from Gods money

Tameness (Acts 5:29) Obedience in all Things

Tenderness (Jeremiah 29:13) Seek God with all your heart

Week 7: Monday	Trusting Jesus

Scripture: Ephesians 5:15-16   Date:

Observation:

Application:

Prayer:

| Week 7: Tuesday | Trusting Jesus |

Scripture: Colossians 3:17   Date:

Observation:

Application:

Prayer:

 YOUR4 Discipleship

Week 7: Wednesday	Trusting Jesus

Scripture: 1 Corinthians 6:19-20   Date:

Observation:

Application:

Prayer:

Week 7: Thursday	Trusting Jesus

Scripture: 1 Corinthians 16:2   Date:

Observation:

Application:

Prayer:

Week 7: Friday	Trusting Jesus

Scripture: Acts 5:29   Date:

Observation:

Application:

Prayer:

Week 7: Saturday	Trusting Jesus
Scripture: Jeremiah 29:13 Date:	
Observation:	
Application:	
Prayer:	

TRIVERGENCE

YOUR4 Convergence is the foundational cornerstone for reaching further into the gospel. During YOUR4 convergence, we dove deeply into understanding our role as a Christian seeking to converge our life with Christ.

We gained a biblical understanding of salvation and expanded our knowledge of how we should answer God's call daily. It is wise to engage with those in whose lives we may have influence. Our existing connections allow space for us to speak into their walk. Our task is not easy. We have learned that it is a gate through which we are to squeeze and filter all decisions through the gospel. Now we realize that Christians are the light that shines into a darkened world, and this light must not be hidden.

Where YOUR4 Convergence laid the foundation of our relationship with Christ, YOUR4 Trivergence picks up and adds another layer through connection. In Trivergence, the body of Christ develops and lives as one in the missional community as we fulfill our calling.

YOUR4 Trivergence will allow us to continue along the

narrow path of learning to be a true disciple of Christ. Topics will include following me, family, and future. These topics ask us to lean into who Christ is and how we are to project Him to the world through our lives and actions. Our mission is to learn to love each person as Christ does. Such love is the core of what the church is to be to this world.

> **³⁹ And the second is like, unto it, thou shalt love thy neighbour as thyself.**
>
> *(Matthew 22:39)*

The only requirement that supersedes the importance of loving our neighbor is to love God. Trivergence equips our heart to see others as Christ sees them—valuable, gifted, and in need of a savior. This stage of our journey will stir the desire within our hearts to love and equip others for the big "K" Kingdom.

PRIORITY CIRCLE 2

Now that we have completed hiking through convergence, it is time to evaluate our hearts about what we learned. The priority circle is an unbiased personal look at how we prioritize life and Christ's calling. It is not a test but rather an opportunity to assess our heart's progress and to discern how far we have traveled down the discipleship trail.

> ²³*Keep thy heart with all diligence; for out of it are the issues of life. Proverbs 4:23*

Every Christian walk should begin with a thorough evaluation of the heart.

Do not fill in what you think is correct. Fill in how you currently see life. The center being #1 priority in your life as you work outwards. To correctly complete, you will need to understand the following: How you spend time, money, and emotional capital.

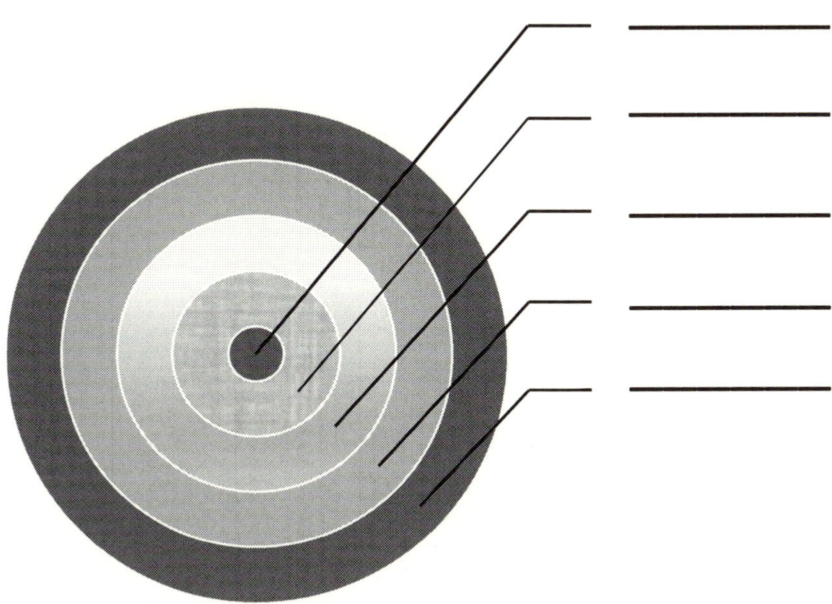

TIME STUDY - 2

Evaluation of our time also points us in the direction of crushing the statement, "I don't have time." If you track your day in round numbers, say from 6 in the morning until 11 at night; where do you spend your time? This must be an honest evaluation between you and God. (Example: Up at 6, work from 7-4, Cook 5-6, TV 6-10, Ready for Bed 11) This can be simple if you are like me, and most days are the same. Complete this for an average day. Have you started to adjust your time around God through convergence?

TASK TITLE	Time Hours

WEEK 8 FOLLOW ME
CHRIST INVITATION COMMUNION

Throughout this journey we are starting to understand Christ desire to be close to us yet allowing us to decide. In John 17:22-24 Christ reveals His desire to be one with us. He went so far as to offer the glory the Father gave Him to us. Oh, how humbling this should be, that the great I Am wants to be one with us. This week during soap time contemplate the whole meaning of who Christ is and what He desires for all that come to know Him.

> A WHOLE NEW GENERATION HAS COME UP BELIEVING THAT IT IS POSSIBLE TO 'ACCEPT' CHRIST WITHOUT FORSAKING THE WORLD."
>
> AW Tozer

Weekly Actions

- S.O.A.P. verses below concerning Christ Invitation
- Call one person from YOUR4 group (We can ask how they are doing, or ask for a prayer request, and so on).

Weekly Scripture

1. 1 Timothy 2:5-7   1 Corinthians 1:10
2. Psalm 34:17-18
3. Romans 12:1-2
4. Ephesians 4:17-19
5. 2 Peter 2:21-23
6. Luke 9:23

Week 8: Monday	Follow Me (Christ)

Scripture: 1 Timothy 2:5-7   Date:

Observation:

Application:

Prayer:

 YOUR4 Discipleship

Week 8: Tuesday	Follow Me (Christ)

Scripture: Psalm 34:17-18   Date:

Observation:

Application:

Prayer:

Week 8: Wednesday	Follow Me (Christ)
Scripture: Romans 12:1-2 Date:	
Observation:	
Application:	
Prayer:	

Week 8: Thursday	Follow Me (Christ)

Scripture: Ephesians 4:17-19   Date:

Observation:

Application:

Prayer:

Week 8: Friday	Follow Me (Christ)

Scripture: 2 Peter 2:21-23   Date:

Observation:

Application:

Prayer:

Week 8: Saturday	Follow Me (Christ)

Scripture: Luke 9:23   Date:

Observation:

Application:

Prayer:

ONE BODY

12 For as the body is one and hath many members, and all the members of that one body, being many, are one body: so also, is Christ.13 For by one Spirit are we all baptized into one body, whether we be Jews or Gentiles, whether we be bond or free; and have been all made to drink into one Spirit. 14 For the body is not one member, but many. 15 If the foot says, Because I am not the hand, I am not of the body; is it therefore not of the body? 16 And if the ear shall say, Because I am not the eye, I am not of the body; is it therefore not of the body? 17 If the whole body were an eye, where were the hearing? If the whole were hearing, where were the smelling? 18 But now hath God set the members every one of them in the body, as it hath pleased him. 19 And if they were all one member, where were the body? 20 But now are they many members, yet but one body. 21 And the eye cannot say unto the hand, I have no need of thee: nor again the head to the feet, I have no need of you. 22 Nay, much more those members of the body, which seem to be more feeble, are necessary: 23 And those members of the body, which we think to be less honourable, upon these we bestow more abundant honour; and our uncomely parts have more abundant comeliness. 24 For our comely parts have no need: but God hath tempered the body together, having given more abundant honour to that part which lacked. 25 That there should be no schism in the body; but that the members should have the same care one for another. 26 And whether one member suffer, all the members suffer with it; or one member be honoured, all the members rejoice with it. 27 Now ye are the body of Christ and members in particular.

(1 Corinthians 12:12-27)

 YOUR4 Discipleship

WEEK 9 LIVING LIFE TOGETHER
Community

Starting this work of outward participation by learning to show love to every man, woman, and child is at the core of hiking Mount Trivergence. This session will encourage us to question a few sacred walls, you know the rituals we have created and placed before God's calling. We will ask questions such as: Why has the call to be one body disappeared? Have the gatekeepers of Christianity allowed large gatherings to snuff out the relational community? This week, as we complete the weekly actions, I encourage each one to reach out with even more vigor. Let us take a short break from hiking and sit around the campfire with friends and strangers.

Weekly Actions

S.O.A.P. verses below concerning Friends

Call or text one from <u>Your4</u>-Their Journey (scripture, encouragement, weekly scripture

Weekly Scripture

1. Share burdens - Galatians 6:1-2
2. Confess to one another - James 5:16
3. Love one another - 1 Peter 4:7-8
4. Submit to one another - Ephesians 5:21
5. Togetherness - Hebrews 10:25
6. Fellowship - Acts 2:42

*"Do not waste time bothering
whether you 'love' your
neighbor; act as if you did."
– C.S. Lewis,*

Mere Christianity

Week 9: Monday	Friends (Life Together)

Scripture: Galatians 6:1-2   Date:

Observation:

Application:

Prayer:

Week 9: Tuesday	Friends (Life Together)

Scripture: James 5:16   Date:

Observation:

Application:

Prayer:

<table>
<tr><td>Week 9: Wednesday</td><td>Friends (Life Together)</td></tr>
</table>

Scripture: 1 Peter 4:7-8   Date:

Observation:

Application:

Prayer:

Week 9: Thursday	Friends (Life Together)

Scripture: Ephesians 5:21   Date:

Observation:

Application:

Prayer:

Week 9: Friday	Friends (Life Together)

Scripture: Hebrews 10:25   Date:

Observation:

Application:

Prayer:

Week 9: Saturday	Friends (Life Together)

Scripture: Acts 2:42   Date:

Observation:

Application:

Prayer:

WEEK 10 CULTURE AROUND US
COMMISSION

<u>Weekly Actions</u>

Coffee Talk

Bring one S.O.A.P. from week 9

<u>Weekly Scripture</u>

1. Acts 1:8
2. Matthew 28:18-20
3. 1 Samuel 16:17
4. Romans 6:17
5. 2 Corinthians 5:11
6. 2 Corinthians 5:13-15

| Week 10: Monday | All Cultures |

Scripture: Acts 1:8   Date:

Observation:

Application:

Prayer:

Week 10: Tuesday	All Cultures

Scripture: Matthew 28:18-20 Date:

Observation:

Application:

Prayer:

| Week 10: Wednesday | All Cultures |

Scripture: 1 Samuel 16:17   Date:

Observation:

Application:

Prayer:

Week 10: Thursday	All Cultures

Scripture: Romans 6:16-17   Date:

Observation:

Application:

Prayer:

Week 10: Friday	All Cultures

Scripture: 2 Corinthians 5:11   Date:

Observation:

Application:

Prayer:

Week 10: Saturday	All Cultures

Scripture: 2 Corinthians 5:13-15   Date:

Observation:

Application:

Prayer:

[16] Thus saith the LORD, stand ye in the ways, and see, and ask for the old paths, where is the good way, and walk therein, and ye shall find rest for your souls. But they said, we will not walk therein.

Jeremiah 6:16

WEEK 11 REMAIN STEADFAST

Throughout the past ten weeks, we invested time understanding Discipleship. This week, we lean into launching our ministry. After completing the 3rd priority circle and time study, we are encouraged to go back and compare them to earlier versions. This will help us understand our progress toward submitting to God. In the coming months, I encourage each one to revisit the priority circle/time study to gauge if we are staying on task and remaining steadfast. If we step away from what we have learned, our priorities will return to what they were when we began our journey. The lack of success is generally due to failing to let God have control. That is, we cannot move forward if we are unwilling to submit fully to Christ and His calling on our life. Learning the hard lesson of letting God have control takes time and much hard work, but we can do this and be victorious.

This week we work to understand God's Word regarding remaining steadfast. As we S.O.A.P. this week, think about how many hurting people watch us for encouragement. Our fall affects more than ourselves; it affects everyone around us daily.

Now that we have summitted Mount Trivergence, we aim to stay in shape for our next adventure.

<u>Weekly Actions</u>

- S.O.A.P. verses below concerning Remain Steadfast
- Call or text one from Your4-Their Journey (scripture, encouragement, etc.)

1. <u>Weekly Scripture</u>1 Corinthians 15:58
2. 2 Peter 1:5-8
3. Galatians 6:9
4. James 1:12
5. James 1:2-4

Isaiah 40:31

<table>
<tr><td>Week 11: Monday</td><td>Remain Steadfast</td></tr>
</table>

Scripture: 1 Corinthians 15:58   Date:

Observation:

Application:

Prayer:

Week 11: Tuesday	Remain Steadfast

Scripture: 2 Peter 1:5-8   Date:

Observation:

Application:

Prayer:

<table>
<tr><td>Week 11: Wednesday</td><td>Remain Steadfast</td></tr>
</table>

Scripture: Galatians 6:9   Date:

Observation:

Application:

Prayer:

Week 11: Thursday	Remain Steadfast

Scripture: James 1:12   Date:

Observation:

Application:

Prayer:

<table>
<tr><td>Week 11: Friday</td><td>Remain Steadfast</td></tr>
</table>

Scripture: James 1:2-4   Date:

Observation:

Application:

Prayer:

Week 11: Saturday	Remain Steadfast

Scripture: Isaiah 40:31 Date:

Observation:

Application:

Prayer:

WEEK 12 REACHING FURTHER

Going through YOUR4 could have taken place anywhere in the world. From our hometowns to a mission field in a foreign land. Regardless of our current location, a real mission always starts wherever our front door is.-Although our front door may change, the mission never does; we are to "Go." This is our opportunity to be on mission every day of every week, whether at home or afar. This week we look at what the Bible says about being on a mission and how this should impact our lives daily. There is no stopping us now as we leave the summit and head home. The adventure has just begun.

¹⁶ for I am not ashamed of the gospel of Christ: for it is the power of God unto salvation to everyone that believeth; to the Jew first, and also to the Greek.

Romans 1:16

Weekly Actions

- S.O.A.P. verses below concerning Remain Steadfast
- Pray out loud with Core Members
- Call or text one from <u>Your4</u>-Their Journey (scripture, encouragement, etc.)
- Coffee Talk with Group Bring a S.O.A.P. Card, or we can discuss our priority/time study if we desire
    - Start preparing to lead Coffee Talk

1. <u>Weekly Scripture </u>Isaiah 6:8
2. 2 Peter 2:15-17
3. Ecclesiastes 4:10-12
4. Mark 5:19-20
5. Mark 16:15-16
6. 1 Corinthians 3:10-15

Week 12: Monday	Reaching Further
Scripture: Isaiah 6:8 Date:	
Observation:	
Application:	
Prayer:	

Week 12: Tuesday	Reaching Further

Scripture: 2 Peter 2:15-17   Date:

Observation:

Application:

Prayer:

Week 12: Wednesday	Reaching Further

Scripture: Ecclesiastes 4:10-12   Date:

Observation:

Application:

Prayer:

Week 12: Thursday	Reaching Further

Scripture: Mark 5:19-20 Date:

Observation:

Application:

Prayer:

Week 12: Friday	Reaching Further

Scripture: Mark 16:15-16 Date:

Observation:

Application:

Prayer:

Week 12: Saturday	Reaching Further

Scripture: 1 Corinthians 3:10-15 Date:

Observation:

Application:

Prayer:

CROSSROADS
YOUR4 Trivergence Conclusion

Throughout YOUR4 Discipleship Hiking, answers were provided regarding the Christian life and calling. Still, others remain to be unearthed. To thrust us forward in our search for answers, part two Climbing follows. Climbing will provide some background to the YOUR4 method and how this stepwise approach has placed us in the position to succeed in Discipleship. Some of the teachings in part 2 will require that we seek clarity concerning the body of Christ and what we have been historically taught. Staying involved and learning through Life Together, is crucial if we want to impact the world for Christ. Failing to participate in the relational community is unhealthy for our walk. Our fallen nature always desires this world and its offerings. Still, the glorious love of God is more precious than anything this world has to offer. The love that washes our hearts and cleanses our souls, leaving us with genuine hope and peace in the present and future, requires Christ. Charles Spurgeon once told the story below of a heart entirely given over to God. This is the heart to strive after each day as we approach God's throne.

"A quiet conscience is a little heaven. A martyr was fastened to the stake, and the sheriff who was to execute him expressed his sorrow that he should persevere in his opinions and compel him to set fire to the pile. The martyr answered, 'Do not trouble yourself, for I am not troubling myself. Come and lay your hand upon my heart and see if it does not beat quietly.' His request was complied with, and he was found to be quite calm. 'Now,' said he, 'lay your hand on your own heart, and see if you are not more troubled than I am; and then go your way, and, instead of pitying me, pity yourself.'" (Spurgeon [3])

FINAL MUSINGS: NOW WHAT?

The last twelve weeks prepared us for the mission field in ways that are not apparent without revealing the method employed. Each S.O.A.P. verse was explicitly designed to point us to a critical finding. If we link/list all the key S.O.A.P. findings together, they point directly to a disciple's life outline. This is seen clearly in week twelve's keywords: 1) Calling 2) Testimony 3) Unity 4) Proclaim at Home 5) Proclaim Abroad 6) Foundations and Rewards.

I would love to see each week's S.O.A.P. list from the twelve-week hiking trail. Not only did the S.O.A.P. direct us, but throughout the program, we composed our discipleship teacher's manual. The S.O.A.P.S and forms completed, the priority circles and the time studies are pieces of the puzzle that, when assembled, reveals how to teach others. Not only is the book work completed.

---

[3] The Metropolitan Tabernacle Pulpit: Sermons, Parts 417-428, page 165

Also, are the simple actions of texting, calling, praying, and coffee talks, which prepared us to be an outspoken missionary of the gospel.

The next steps should be evident in the YOUR4 we listed in week six and worked to develop relationally in weeks 7-12. Gather your YOUR4 for an introductory coffee talk, inviting others to participate in a YOUR4 journey. Remember that we have created an awesome community, so use it as a resource as we launch our own YOUR4.

Purchase YOUR4 Discipleship at Amazon.com. Get started on the calling of Christ and Go ye, therefore.

YOUR4 Ministries would love to share in your list of keywords from the daily S.O.A.P.S. Share your hiking journey through Mount Convergence and Mount Trivergence, allowing us to rejoice within the body of Christ for your accomplishments.

Connect with us online at:

www.YOUR4.net

Email: brettbodiford@hotmail.com

Subject: YOUR4 Discipleship

YOUR4 Ministries is available for engagements such as: Preaching, Conferences, Church Leadership consults regarding YOUR4 Discipleship, etc.

PART 2

YOUR4 DISCIPLESHIP CLIMBING

³ Call unto me, and I will answer thee, and show thee great and mighty things, which thou knowest not.

Jeremiah 33:3

1 BEING THE SHERPA

Out of the excitement of God's revelation in my life, YOUR4 Discipleship was born. It did not arise as a finished work but rather as a work in progress. My prayer is that throughout our Journey, we will lean into God and His desire for our happiness, hope, and peace. Discipleship through YOUR4 will encourage and provide a zeal to follow in Christ's footsteps. The path we follow will enhance our Christian walk and turn the world upside down as the early Christian church. *"These that have turned the world upside down are come hither also"* (Acts 17:6b)

The objective is to understand how we are the light that shines into a darkened world. Hiking Mt. Convergence laid the basics for the program and brought full Discipleship into focus. Now, as we start the last section of YOUR4 Climbing, we seek to understand the methods and applications. With the goal being to see people as Christ sees them and to move them into a relationship with Christ.

Our hearts will telescope the gospel that we live. Looking through the lens of Christ, we discover the potential for the gospel to shine light into a darkened world through our testimony. This telescopic, Christ-centered lens will expand our horizons by feeding the desire to love others as Christ loves us. Peering through a Christ-centered telescope, the darkness we see will break our hearts and burden our soul.

During our Hiking experience, we planted seeds that now must be watered so God can receive the increase.

6 I have planted, Apollos watered; but God gave the increase.

7 So then neither is he that planteth any thing, neither he that watereth, but God that giveth the increase. 8 Now he that planteth and he that watereth are one: and every man shall receive his own reward according to his own labour.

(1 Corinthians 3:6-8)

Serving as light to the world represents a way of life. Without the love of Christ shining into dark places, how else will people come to know Christ? God has called Christians to be part of the change. Statistics speak to the darkness that has enveloped the world.

- 78% of the unchurched would listen to someone who shared what they believed about Christianity. [4]

- 3 out of 4 Christians (74%) seldom have a "spiritual conversation" with anyone.[5]

- More than 50% of all Evangelicals believe there is more than one way to Heaven.[6]

- 75% of regular church attenders do not believe that sharing their faith is important.[7]

-

Christians, therefore, must step up their vigilance when it comes to witnessing for Christ. It is time to take up the baton and run the race set before us.

Wherefore seeing we also are compassed about with so great a cloud of witnesses, let us lay aside every weight and the sin which doth so easily beset us, and let us run with patience the race that is set before us, [2] Looking unto Jesus the author and finisher of our faith; who for the joy that was set before him endured the cross, despising the shame, and is set down at the right hand of the throne of God.

(Hebrews 12:1-2)

Our races begin by taking the first step in pursuit of the finish line. There, at the finish line, Christ awaits arms opened wide, saying: [21] *...Well done, thou good and faithful servant: thou hast been faithful over a few things, I will make thee ruler over many things: enter*

---

[4] Lifeway Research
[5] Spiritual Conversations in the Digital Age, Barna Group, 2018
[6] U.S. Religious Landscape Study, Pew Research Center, 2014
[7] State of American Theology, 2014

thou into the joy of thy lord. Matthew 25:21. Imagine the joyous reunion as we approach the end of our race and see our Savior in the distance. We must keep our eyes and hearts trained on that great and glorious day to overcome all that we experience on earth.

Therefore, as we move forward, each of us must evaluate our hearts regarding God, family, friends, and the future. Our goal is to provide relational ministry as we seek to become the body of Christ. We do this through our service as a community of believers (church), living together, crying together, and sorting life experiences together. Through YOUR4, then, let us reclaim the gospel fire for all of mankind in our home, outside our doors, and abroad. We must do this in remembrance of what we are called to do as Christ's disciples on each step of our journey.

2 ENEMY OF THE CHURCH
CHEAP GRACE

Christ led me to evaluate my spiritual direction. I gazed forward to reflect on where the institutional church was headed and who was following its course. My reflections led to discoveries that were heartbreaking and eye-opening. That is, the mantra of the modern-day church has become gather people by any means necessary. Please understand this statement or discussion is not inclusive of all churches. I love church. In fact, I am a part of the church or body of Christ just as all believers. But gathering people together by any means or lowering the standards that Christians are called to uphold damages the body of Christ. This is a cause for concern.

On the one hand, it does not matter if we gather in small groups, missional communities, or any other form. On the other hand, what we do when we gather matters. If we are not attentive to what we do when we gather, we risk offering new converts, at best, a cheap imitation of the Christian life. At worst, leaving them to figure out the nuances of living as a Christian on their own. Leaving them to their own desires and guidance will end in failing to accomplish God's calling and usually a defeated Christian life.

After a person becomes a Christian, the Holy Spirit instills in him or her a spirit of conviction that drives an internal desire to walk in Discipleship with the body of Christ. That desire requires feeding and nurturing by the larger body or bodies. This type of nurturing love is only found among other Christians, be it small groups, relational ministries, or extensive worship services. A new Christian's desire may be fragile, at best, and therefore it must be watered with the Word and cared for by other Christians. In the absence of proper care and feeding of the new convert, he or she is at risk of becoming trapped by cheap grace. As Dietrich Bonhoeffer puts it in, *The Cost of Discipleship* (1937):

> *Cheap grace is the preaching of forgiveness without requiring repentance, baptism without church discipline, Communion without confession, absolution without personal confession. Cheap grace is grace without discipleship, grace without the cross, grace without Jesus Christ, living, and incarnate.*[8]*(emphasis added).*

God's church, or "the body," should never allow cheap grace to be an option; the provision of the alternative is worth any price it must pay. The body of Christ must ensure full grace. They should provide discipleship that enables converts to strike out victoriously.

---

[8] Dietrich Bonhoeffer, The Cost of Discipleship, page 44-45

As God works out YOUR4 in my life, I have noticed a directional shift as I develop YOUR4 Discipleship. This shift guides me away from cheap grace. In the absence of a new direction and method, a true north, if you will, we would be doomed to peddle cheap grace in the future as well.

Offering cheap grace to Christians impairs their progression toward becoming fully equipped and armored warriors. Such warriors are in high demand as they are the ones Christ calls into a darkened world to shed the light of hope. Therefore, we must prepare ourselves as a body to disseminate the Word amongst the enemy forces of darkness. The success of our mission relies on the elimination of cheap grace from the Christian community. Cheap grace stunts the growth and development of the body rendering it insufferably immature and insufficiently potent. In other words, such immaturity in the form of cheap grace maligns the efficacy of the teaching we are called to do. It impairs our ability to recruit and train disciples. That is why the body must declare in unison, "The time is now to turn back to the Full Grace of Christ and create disciples eager to follow in His footsteps, no matter the cost or the cross.

BENEFITS OF FULL GRACE

We must look forward and backward to see where we are headed and to see who is following. Imagine, for a moment, Christians who accept Full Grace. These Christians will have a desire to serve the Lord not only in the church but in daily life. They will eagerly accept grace that is wholly ripened and full of that sweet flavor of release from past wounds. They will approach Christ with total abandon, withholding nothing. Seeking to live Christ-centered love so completely their sinful flesh will convulse as their commitment to Christ conquers it. Such longing on the part of Christians will generate hearts that cling to Christ with nail breaking tenacity.

Full grace becomes a salve for all wounds, even those that are self-inflicted. Ultimately, full grace as Christ showed us, will obliterate the cheap grace offered by the disjointed and misguided branches of the body.

Transitioning from cheap grace to full grace will create change. First, Christians will recognize heartbreak not only as physical but also as spiritual during encounters with the hurting. Second, the pain of others will become palpable to the Christ-centered heart. Third, one desires for others to experience the same love and forgiveness they received. Fourth, a Christian will live as a disciple on mission and in community.

Disciples in Christ require community. We cannot do our work alone. Learning to live in communion with Christ in community with others, and in commission to those in the culture, transforms us. This relational community fuels hearts with an urgency to help others come to Christ before it is too late.

> [24] *And let us consider one another to provoke unto love and to good works:*[25] *Not forsaking the assembling of ourselves together, as the manner of some is but exhorting one another: and so much the more, as ye see the day approaching. (Hebrews 10:24-25).*

Hebrews 10:24-25 is relevant today because of what it says about Full Grace and its importance for all converts.

To *"stir up one another"* is to invite one another to love and engage in good works. We must encourage one another on our walks as disciples of Christ. <u>By _"not neglecting meeting together,"_</u> we are less likely to fall prey to discouragement and isolation.

When we <u>_"encourage one another"_</u> through our attendance at missional gatherings, for instance, we both support and encourage those with whom we are in a relational community.

Often, we fail to gather because we forget why company and community are valuable aspects of our lives as disciples. When we live in a relational community with others, it is not only for our benefit but also because someone else might need us. Engagement with others in a condition that is infused with a sense of urgency is _"all the more_ [important] _as we see the day drawing near."_ That is, our calling to live with urgency to reach those who have not responded to the gospel or who do not know the truth.

Thus, conversion is much more than a prayer or a gathering. Instead, conversion offers entry into Life Together, wherein we collectively embrace Christ in The Body.

152

3 CONVERGENCE-TRIVERGENCE:
WHAT?

YOUR4 Hiking is broken into two sessions: convergence and trivergence. Convergence takes a deep dive into our personal journey of becoming one with God. The basics of our Christianity and discipleship were developed by creating personal study, alone time with God, and the commencement of relational community. Convergence sought to center our lives, creating harmony with Christ and His mission for life. This deep dive uncovers that a true convergence with Christ requires all of who we are to surrender. Growing closer to convergence with God opens our eyes to His graciousness and encourages us to share His will.

Trivergence moves us away from the evaluation of ourselves and into action with others. Living out our closeness or convergence with Christ drives our hearts to invite others into relational Christian community. Reaching out to others is an enormous step for most Christians. Yet any fear felt can be overcome with a quick review of the step's convergence provided and a review of S.O.A.P. applications and prayers from our notebooks. The trivergence hike takes us on a more challenging trail but nothing we cannot handle.

Seeking and leading others into a relationship with Christ is our part in growing the body of Christ. Trivergence is a requirement because Christ did not call us to be alone. God's design is for us to live together as one body on mission.

YOUR4 Hiking allows us to backtrack our discipleship journey. This layout equips each one to lead the next YOUR4 Discipleship group. As we traveled the hiking trails, taking notes, we were writing our own leadership guide.

Remember, we are called to "Go" create disciples who create disciples. Let us start climbing and consider how each step of our hiking trail has conditioned us for the next step in the journey.

WHO WILL THE JOURNEY BENEFIT?

This journey is for people seeking to successfully motivate themselves toward the mission of being on mission while walking as Christ did during His Earthly ministry. Christ's Earthly ministry was born of a love for everyone who could not attain love and care without His sacrifice. He came humbly, loving the unlovable, of which I am one. As we study the footsteps of Christ, the calling for our life becomes clear. As Christians, we become the hands and feet Jesus ask us to be reaching the world by shining Jesus' loving light on those in need. Not only those in need of physical healing but also, and most importantly, spiritual healing. This is our duty as Christians, but it ought to be our hearts' desire to reach those whom society has forgotten or written off. We find our treasure in those whom others view as outcasts. As the founder of the mission, "Inca Linc," Rich Brown says, our mission involves "reaching the lost, the least, and the last." The categories include those who do not know Christ, those deemed the "least" by society, and the last one saved before Christ returns. Let us embark on YOUR4 Discipleship to realize Christ's vision as we travel in His footsteps to find "that one."

10 For the Son of man is come to seek and to save that which was lost. Luke 19:10

YOUR4 Discipleship seeks those who are the least, the lost, and the last. Ultimately, we will create disciples who come to understand: How God loves, who God is, and what God's eternal grace offers. Your4 Discipleship should encourage and enlighten us to follow Christ's path, especially when the journey leads us to our cross.

23 And he said to them all, If any man will come after me, let him deny himself, and take up his cross daily, and follow me. Luke 9:23

Your4 creates a pathway for the fulfillment of our calling to spread the gospel and share the grace God bestows on mankind as a gift. The body of Christ is not called to a building alone. Instead, we are called to Christ, to one another, and to those we meet in our going. The building, missional community, or small group arise out of love for Christ and from a desire to be part of the Body in the right relationship before Christ.

*¹⁶**Let your light so shine before men** that they may see your good works and glorify your Father which is in heaven.* *Matthew 5:16 (KJV)*

*¹⁹ **Go ye therefore**, and teach all nations, baptizing them in the name of the Father, and of the Son, and the Holy Ghost: ²⁰Teaching them to observe all things whatsoever I have commanded you: (Matthew 28:19-20)*

YOUR4 Discipleship is immersive and interactive, thus allowing us to live out and embrace the three Pillars of Communion: with God, in community with others, and in commission to those around us. The three pillars represent the essence of ministry and signify how we should work within our sphere of influence and beyond.

- **<u>Communion</u> with God**
  ²⁸ Come unto me, all ye that labour and are heavy laden, and I will give you rest. ²⁹ Take my yoke upon you and learn of me; for I am meek and lowly in heart: and ye shall find rest unto your souls. ³⁰ For my yoke is easy, and my burden is light. (Mt. 11-28-30)

- **<u>Community</u> with others**
  ³⁷ Jesus said unto him, thou shalt love the Lord thy God with all thy heart, and with all thy soul, and with all thy mind. ³⁸ This is the first and great commandment. ³⁹And the second is like unto it, thou shalt love thy neighbour as thyself. ⁴⁰On these two commandments hang all the law and the prophets. (Mt. 22:37-40)

- **<u>Commission</u>** to the culture around us
  [19] Go ye therefore, and teach all nations, baptizing them in the name of the Father, and of the Son, and the Holy Ghost: (Mt. 28:19)

How do Christians grow through YOUR4 Discipleship?

Discipleship solidifies Gods calling on our life. Utilizing the framework from the 70-20-10 approach. Enhancing development through:

Communion Community & Commission

The learning model throughout YOUR4 is based on the framework of the 70-20-10 model of learning.

- Personal assignments/challenges (70%)
- Developing relationships (20%)
- Expanded training (10%)

YOUR4 Discipleship percentages will not be as evenly spaced as 70-20-10 as our focus is on Christ and His leading. These corporate concepts are worthy of consideration in disciple-making as much as in leadership development. The 70-20-10 method is geared toward lasting change regarding our approaches to ministry and living in line with what we learn. Fill in the blanks type learning with no responsibility for action has not proven effective in my experience. Most people fill in the blanks with the correct answer but fail to internalize the associated lesson. The fill-in-the-blank method neither touches the heart nor leads to a bold proclamation of Christ to the least, the last, and the lost

The corporate model suggests that at least 70% of our lessons come from hands-on challenges. YOUR4 discipleship incorporated such challenges in the form of daily S.O.A.P.S, weekly private actions, and public actions. The most significant change in anyone's life will inevitably come from spending time in God's Word, seeking His will, and spending one-on-one time in prayer. Personal devotional time cultivates a personal relationship with the Father and aides in restructuring one's life to be submitted to the one and only Lord.

The 20% portion refers to the time we spend with other Christians in a relational community participating in both support and mentoring. This 20% teaches that God did not call us to serve ourselves but to serve others. We are to support one another throughout life. Every person upholds another while being upheld. Today, we may be a mentor, whereas tomorrow, we may be the mentee. Everyone needs support, and this happens as the body of Christ unifies.

The last 10% expands the group and takes place in a more formalized setting such as Life Together (small groups), preaching services, retreats, and class time. This model provides experience in each facet of discipleship. Thus, it equips us with a complete set of tools, preparing us to be more than spectators. As we incorporate the 70-20-10 approach, we must understand that this phase is not completed unique to one another but are entwined together as we work our way through YOUR4.

COMMUNION: LEARNING BY DOING: 70%

As mentioned above, the most considerable portion of our time will be spent with hands-on challenges. For many, these challenges will be new experiences that foster new learning. This learning may be growing closer to God through prayer and bible study. This alone time is meant as a tool to reset our routine and create a regular rhythm of serving Christ through a personal relationship with Him.

As we journey further into communion, we start to understand the immense change that takes place when crises arise in our life. No longer do we react as those who do not know Christ, but we take each situation to Christ for direction.

The 70% builds a personal relationship inspiring us to give each part of our life to Him. This step is crucial because each thing we learn to give to Christ will grow us to help others along the way.

The other challenging task about a personal relationship built around dedicated time to Christ is just that, time. The number one answer I get when asking if someone reads their Bible is, "I do not have time." This only points out that most people I talk with have put God at the back of the line. Our learning must start with the most significant percentage being devoted to the realignment of our priorities. If we do not have time for God, how do we expect to encourage others to live a victorious life? Realignment requires admitting to God that we have placed Him last until a crisis arose. At the crisis point, everyone has time for prayer. He must always be included in all places and all decisions. This correct standing will bolster our faith and dependence on Christ, growing us to be more Christlike in every facet of life. The personal 70% should challenge us through new experiences with God, and new reflections on life.

As we enhance our relationship with Christ, we will be driven to share the good news with those who do not know. We will also be sharing life together with the ones living victoriously.

THE 70% LEARNING OF COMMUNION

Communion encourages and challenges us to seek more in-depth answers to questions such as:

1. Why do I believe what I believe?
2. What is God saying through His Word?
3. What do I do with God's Word daily?
4. How do I apply God's Word to my life?

Communion not only encourages questions, but it also enables boldness through actions such as:

1. Discovery of oneself as we consider Christ
2. Refinement of our spiritual thinking
3. Assistance tackling issues and tasks in a Godly manner
4. Using biblical principles & actions in all situations

COMMUNITY: LEARNING FROM AND INVESTING IN OTHERS THE 20%

Time spent with other Christians as part of a discipling program plays a vital role in the relational community. Christlike behavior toward others, whether saved or lost, is established through community. We are to spend time together discussing our lives, fears, hopes, and dreams. These types of deep conversations must be nurtured. This nurturing relationship will create an environment that is conducive to trust with even our darkest secrets.

Most human behavior is learned through observation; that is, we learn by modeling others' behavior, good or bad. We act and react based on conduct that has been modeled by others for us. In Bandura's social learning theory, he states,

"Learning would be exceedingly laborious, not to mention hazardous if people had to rely solely on the effects of their actions to inform them what to do. Fortunately, most human behavior is learned observationally through modeling: from observing others, one forms an idea of how new behaviors are performed, and on later occasions, this coded information serves as a guide for action." [9]

This applies to how we learn within the family of God as well. The closer we walk together, the more openly we live our Christian lives. This community learning piece is not applied only to modeling other behaviors. It also holds us accountable for behaviors as others will model our actions. Throughout our Hiking, the three pillars (3Cs) of discipleship were modeled. The modeling should allow us to recognize a need for Retention, Replication, and Motivation. These three aspects comprise the bedrock of the 20% phase of learning.

"[11] If they obey and serve him, they shall spend their days in prosperity and their years in pleasures." (Job 36:11)

- **Retention:** Storage and recall of information may be of concern when learning to share the gospel message with others. But as we have learned, God is faithful in all things, even memory recall. The difference between storing God's Word and other types of data is God will provide a recall mechanism in our time

---

[9] Bandura, A. (1977) Social Learning Theory. New York: General Learning Press. Pg. 22

of need. Spending time with Christ and other Christians facilitates God's provision of this mechanism. The human brain can store unlimited amounts of information. The more stored information is repeated or used, the more likely it will be saved and easily recalled. Although, if there are disorders of the brain or trauma, the human brain may not remember some memories. This is most evident with Alzheimer's patients. Yet, as I sat and talked with an elderly gentleman that had preached for many years. He told me about the bible, the ministry, and his savior, I was extremely impressed and touched by his passion. Later I learned he had late-stage Alzheimer's. Christ will provide His Word when needed regardless of the flesh and its failings. Although, we can facilitate the daily recall through study and relational ministry that calls us to live out God's Word. Matthew 10:19.

"19 But when they deliver you up, take no thought how or what ye shall speak: for it shall be given you in that same hour what ye shall speak." (Matthew 10:19)

- **Replication:** As we learn through study and personal relationship with Christ, we should be driven to replicate the love we were shown. We are not disciples until we replicate discipleship within another. Investing in someone to lead them to Christ and not only to Him for a confession but to Him for a life change is desired. The desire to share the hope that is found in Christ alone should motivate us each minute. The further we travel along this path; we notice a change that culminates when we let go of our selfish attitudes. We become disciples who see God in every situation and yearn to produce disciples. Throughout the learning process, our priority circle should continue its realignment by placing Christ closer to the center of who we are and what we desire.

> [8] *Herein is my Father glorified, that ye bear much fruit; so, shall ye be my disciples. (John 15:8)*

Motivation: YOUR4 group leaders are great at this as they have experienced God at work. They have learned to be obedient to the calling and are driven to help others. Leaders reinforce, support, and walk with new disciples by answering questions, modeling behaviors, and being a Christian friend. Now that we have completed the hiking portion of YOUR4, we will have a better grasp of who we are in Christ and what excites us. The excitement that is driven by knowing Christ deeply reveals our gifting, and this drives motivation.

There are times when Christians focus on paths without the gifting or calling of God and struggle without excitement or satisfaction. Whereas if we work within our gifting, even the failings will be exciting as we look at the lessons that are moving us forward in God's work. Another motivating factor is the community we built in the YOUR4 journey supporting and encouraging us not to give up.

Equips the disciple for
Encouragement & loving
straightforward feedback.

THE 20% LEARNING OF COMMUNITY

1. Praying Together
2. Peer Interaction
3. Leadership Challenges
4. Activities
5. Coaching
6. Texting
7. Modeling Behavior

LEARNING THROUGH INSTRUCTION: THE 10%

As YOUR4 developed, we were concerned that a misconception could hinder the creation of disciples if we did not address it directly. The framework of YOUR4 and the use of the 70-20-10 approach may appear biased toward the large modern-day gathering. Driving disciples to meet in relational smaller Christian communities may communicate that large crowds are not encouraged. However, the final 10% is learning through gathering with larger groups to hear and learn from teaching. These larger gatherings encourage the disciple to take notes and meditate on more profound truths. As we take notes and study the meaning behind the instruction, we facilitate critical thinking.

The larger gathering structure is another method to grow deeper. It enlightens us to new theology and doctrine and a deeper dive into our YOUR4 group. As we dive deeper, our foundation expands along with our critical thinking and life-changing behaviors within the group. Larger gatherings can be accomplished in varying ways, institutional Church attendance, Life Together groups, conferences, camps, etc. The final 10% adds another layer of depth to our learning and inspires a more active and successful discipleship life.

WHEN…SHOULD I GET STARTED? NOW.

Christ answered immediately when we called out to Him in despair. Saving grace by way of His sacrifice and crucifixion were not delayed even for an instant. If we are to follow Christ, we must evaluate His Word and the answers from our YOUR4 Hiking and Climbing.

Becoming a living copy of Christ should be our heart's desire!

[32] *"Whosoever, therefore, shall confess me before men, him will I confess also before my Father which is in heaven.* [33] *But whosoever shall deny me before men, him will I also deny before my Father which is in heaven." (Matthew 10:32-33)*

[38] *And he that taketh not his cross, and followeth after me is not worthy of me.* [39] *He that findeth his life shall lose it: and he that loseth his life for my sake shall find it.* [40] *He that receiveth you receiveth me, and he that receiveth me receiveth him that sent me." (Matthew 10:38-40)*

The Enduring Word Commentary speaks about taking up the cross as follows:

> *"**Take his cross and follow after Me**: The disciple must follow Jesus even to the place of taking **his cross**. When a person took a cross in Jesus' day, it was for one reason: to die. The ancient Roman cross did not negotiate, did not compromise, and did not make deals. There was no looking back when you took up your cross, and your only hope was in resurrection life."* [10]

After we accept Christ's gift of grace, it is not only our duty but our pleasure to do His will. Shining His light into a darkened world is such an honor, knowing we are messengers of the King. We have won the war even though we continue to battle. It seems incomprehensible that we could misinterpret Matthew chapter 10, verse 38.

The writer's example of the cross as an instrument of death suggests that taking the cross means we are crucified to an earthly life but seek glorification through Christ. As a crucified man, of the "flesh," we no longer feel, hear, or touch, outside of Christ. We die to self to take up our cross in service to Christ; we become less as He becomes more.

[30] He must increase, but I must decrease." John 3:30

Our joy is revealed through death to self and life from the Father. We make Him more visible than ourselves, which is also our goal as we lead others.

---

[10] https://enduringword.com/bible-commentary/matthew-10/

" It is no longer I who live, but Christ who lives in me. And the life I now live in the flesh, I live by faith in the Son of God, who loved me and gave himself for me." Galatians 2:20

We are the Lord's light unto the world. Disciples must be about the Father's business as the darkness of days encroaches on the light. We are approaching the time when witnessing will be complete, and all men will stand before almighty God to be judged.

The interesting aspect of this verse is to take up the cross for Christ. This means that we die a temporary death to our fleshly desires but inherit eternal glory with Christ. If we decide not to take up Christ's cross, Satan will supply a cross that gives us death on earth in spirit and eternal death in hell away from God and love. Do we as Judas run to the Lord saying greetings, Master, and kiss His cheek while living a life that is devoid of Christ? Do we betray Jesus with our hearts while speaking of Him to others with our mouths? Our savior took the cross on our behalf, and now we are called to take the cross on His.

Seeking to serve Christ will cost us in this world's eyes. Studying the Bible will cause division within ourselves as the Bible is disliked by the flesh. Serving Christ is more than crying Master and giving a short kiss on the cheek to identify Him. Serving Christ is taking up one's cross daily, dying to self while living to Christ.

⁵ Love not the world, neither the things that are in the world. If any man loves the world, the love of the Father is not in him. ¹⁶ For all that is in the world, the lust of the flesh, and the lust of the eyes, and the pride of life, is not of the Father but is of the world. ¹⁷ And the world passeth away, and the lust thereof: but he that doeth the will of God abideth forever. 1 John 2:15-17

4 QUALITIES OF A DISCIPLE

"Follow me, and I will make you fishers of men." Matthew 4:19

Discipleship is a word that is batted around like a kid's baseball at the park. What is discipleship? How do we become disciples? Where do we go and live out discipleship? Are disciples only sent overseas to foreign lands? These are some common questions when discussing what, when, and where for disciples. We all think we understand the term, but how many have stopped to study and understand God's commission for our lives? Without a proper understanding of God's commission for the Christian, we can unintentionally absolve ourselves of personal responsibility to the world around us. It is easy to take the word disciple without the study of scripture and misinterpret where we should focus. Many times, the word disciple conjures up the thought of walking in sandals from town to town preaching the gospel. Although, if this is the call from God, it will work. But mostly, the word disciple is our calling to spread the gospel to every man, woman, and child. This responsibility is meant for each individual Christian and not reserved for local church leadership.

WHAT IS A DISCIPLE'S CALL?

Correcting our perception of discipleship through scripture enables the expansion of the body of Christ through a healthy and productive process. Within scripture, there are at least five calls to a disciple lifestyle. Through these five verses, we are given an audience, commission, power, directive, and direction. Let us look at each verse and its instruction for our lives

AUDIENCE

15 And he said unto them, Go ye into all the world, and preach the gospel to every creature. Mark 16:15

Jesus has risen from the dead and tells the disciples to Go into all the world teaching. This statement removes all opportunity for bias to anyone they encountered. Christ has now opened the gospel to every creature in the world. This is still true for us today as well. God has given us an audience that includes each person we encounter. Thus, there is one place we can begin our preparation for discipleship to the world, in the home. Failing to be a Christlike disciple in our homes displays an immaturity in the faith of the believer. How do we speak to strangers with boldness when we cower from speaking the gospel to the ones that we care for the most? Learning boldness in portraying the gospel for friends and family will prepare us for situations with strangers and neighbors. This preparation ensures we love our neighbor as ourselves.

The noble effort of sending disciples to foreign lands from America remains as crucial as ever. Yet, we must realize that today America needs disciples. During the founding of America, Christian values were the standard. Biblical foundations, namely Christ, were the cornerstone. As time passed, Christians lost influence at home and in their communities. The movement to please oneself gained a foothold nationally. It lulled us to sleep regarding our Christian values and life together in our neighborhoods.

Charles Spurgeon, when asked about people falling asleep in church, replied, "Someone should wake up the preacher." The point now applies to America. That is, we have fallen asleep at the wheel regarding discipleship and our concern for those God has called us to love. Spurgeon spoke of waking the preacher, but we must awaken the body of Christ from slumber. America needs each Christian to understand the calling of discipleship to family and community Crossroads Aiken Pastor Jake Edwards put it this way in his sermon from Acts 16: "Discipleship begins at home and ends nowhere."

With this as our backdrop, we must seek every man, woman, and child here and abroad. Today, we can transform our corner of the world through God's two-step process.

37 Jesus said unto him, thou shalt love the Lord thy God with all thy heart, and with all thy soul, and with all thy mind. 38 This is the first and great commandment. 39 And the second is like unto it, thou shalt love thy neighbour as thyself. 40 On these two commandments hang all the law and the prophets. Matthew 22:37-40

At no point, did Christ suggest we put ourselves first. The commission is to love and pray for others while placing God first in our lives. Each of us is a light unto the world. Our responsibility cannot be laid upon any other person, be it the pastor, church, or deacon. If the body of Christ continues to fail at living out Christ's calling to His audience, we will forge our own chains to this world. These chains will choke the life from the believer's voice.

One of the American founding fathers, Patrick Henry, put it this way:

"Bad men cannot make good citizens. It is impossible that a nation of infidels or idolaters should be a nation of free men. It is when a people forget God that tyrants forge their chains."[11]

COMMISSION

21 Then said Jesus to them again, Peace be unto you: as my Father hath sent me, even so send I you. John 20:21

---

[11] Patrick Henry US Founding Father, no source found

As Christ stands before the disciples in verse 20, He showed them the marks in his side and hands. The marks of love for all humanity. The brutality with which He was slain is unimaginable yet is what was required for our salvation and healing. After the resurrection, you would think He would say enough, but that is not who we serve. Christ now commissions all of us to go into the world, telling the good news of His resurrection. Christ states it very clearly that we are being sent to others as God the Father sent Him to us.

In this sending, we should take note Christ showed them the marks of the cross before sending them to the world in His name. We will experience persecution if we stand for Christ. The book of 1 Peter not only describes suffering but the hope that comes with knowing Christ. Our hope is the place setting with our name affixed at the Lord's table. Accepting this commission from Christ requires us to lay aside our fleshly desires and replace them with God's love. Either we set aside materialism and serve Christ or refuse Christ and serve our idols. There is not a way to keep one hand holding to this world and the other to Christ. We have been sent, and the cost displayed by Christ in John 20:20 could be the cost we pay. Are we serving as called by Christ?

> *24 No man can serve two masters: for either he will hate the one and love the other; or else he will hold to the one and despise the other. Ye cannot serve God and mammon. Matthew 6:24*

POWER

> *8 But ye shall receive power, after that the Holy Ghost is come upon you: and ye shall be witnesses unto me both in Jerusalem, and in all Judaea, and in Samaria, and unto the uttermost part of the earth. Acts 1:8*

Acts 1:8 states we will receive power from the Holy Spirit, we are to witness unto Christ, and we are again reminded to go into all the world. It directs each believer to reach and teach everyone across the globe after we are empowered with the spirit. It is not accurate for any servant of the Lord to say they are not called to witness. Our duty is not to direct someone to the preacher for a salvation message. Our personal relationship with Christ and the power of the Holy Spirit is all we need to lead others to hope in Christ. The Believer's Bible Commentary says this about the power spoken of in Acts 1:8.

> *"This power is the grand indispensable of Christian witness. A man may be exceptionally talented, intensively trained, and widely experienced, but without spiritual power, he is ineffective. On the other hand, a man may be uneducated, unattractive, and unrefined, yet let him be endued with the power of the Holy Spirit. The world will turn out to see him burn for God."*[12]

When persecution comes, and it will, we must remember who our partner is on the battlefield. The Holy Spirit is ever with us, no matter the circumstance. The power we need for ministry already lives within us.

MESSAGE

> [47] *And that repentance and remission of sins should be preached in his name among all nations, beginning at Jerusalem. Luke 24:47*

This portion of scripture is difficult to parse out from the

---

[12] Believer's Bible Commentary second edition. Thomas Nelson, pg. 1551

rest of the chapter. Christ is giving the disciples (us) a new message that can now be preached in His name. Before Christ fulfilled the scripture, through His death, burial, and resurrection, salvation through grace could not be preached. Christ, having now filled the Father's will anyone who gets to Heaven will do so through the blood of Jesus. Our message is presented to us very clearly, repentance, and remission of sins through Jesus Christ, our Lord. There may be many with doctorates and degrees. Still, anyone endued with the power of the Holy Spirit can preach what changed in their lives through salvation. Anyone can explain the faith, hope, and love permeating every part of their being after surrendering to the Master. Christ ensured that the message was accessible to everyone.

SUMMARY OF OUR COMMISSION

> *¹⁹ Go ye therefore, and teach all nations, baptizing them in the name of the Father, and of the Son, and of the Holy Ghost:*
> *²⁰ Teaching them to observe all things whatsoever I have commanded you: and, lo, I am with you always, even unto the end of the world. Amen. Matthew 28:19-20*

Now that we have covered four of the five commission verses, the final two verses sum up the fact that God is sending each believer to make disciples.

"Go ye therefore" or in your daily going.

"Teach all nations" or make disciples of each believer.

"Teaching them…all things whatsoever I have commanded you" or teach them what you know from God.

The word "go" in verse 19 is not directed at everyone in the world. This word is directed to the one endued with the power of the Holy Spirit. In Acts 1:8, we learned that after salvation, we will be given power. Acts 1:8 only directs us to go after each believer receives this power at repentance. The follower of Christ will go and carry the message of hope because of the indwelling power of the Holy Spirit. If we feel no desire to tell others about Christ, stop and talk with God in prayer, as I am personally concerned about your spiritual relationship with Christ. This does not mean we are to run around, yelling Christ's message at the top of our lungs to everyone we encounter. Still, we should be broken-hearted for those that do not know the truth to the point that we look for the opportunity to invest intentionally.

The second statement to "teach all nations" can be translated "make disciples." We must understand that we cannot save anyone. We are used as instruments of God and live our faith out in a way that points people to Christ. After salvation, we are to invest with what knowledge we gained studying and relational ministry through our YOUR4 groups to the new Christian.

Baptizing comes immediately after salvation as a means of indicating our repentance or turning away from sin. This does not mean we will never sin, but when we turn to Christ in submission, sin will bother the heart and soul of the true believer.

"Teaching them to observe all things whatsoever I have commanded you." This verse is our call to intentional investment in utilizing our knowledge of Christ. Of course, we do not know everything, but we do know some things. Use this to open dialogue and learning opportunities. Not only did Christ send the Holy Spirit to live within us, but verse 20 it states He is always with us. Stop being fearful. We serve the King of all that is and all that will be.

In summary, I would like to paraphrase verses 19 and 20 as follows: As we are going, make disciples, baptizing and teaching them everything I taught you. The final two verses sum up the other four calls to commission. We have a roadmap after conversion. We immediately have an audience, a calling, power, and a new message to share. Go love others as Christ loves us.

TANGIBLE QUALITIES OF DISCIPLES

Upon completing Your4 Discipleship, we will recognize the call to love others. This love is to be conferred empathetically and spiritually. Learning to love others in tangible ways will allow the disciple to reach into people's lives with Christ's love. This reaching will require compassion for each person with whom we come into contact, identification with Christ through our actions, and faith in the power given through salvation. As we invest in others, it will become apparent that the internal eight qualities will need continual food for growth. These eight qualities were shown throughout Jesus' earthly ministry as He touched the ones the world despised and encouraged those the world attacked.

TANGIBLE TOUCH OF COMPASSION

In Matthew 8:3, Christ touches a leper: "And Jesus put forth His hand and touched him" (Mt 8:3). When Christ touches the leper, the leper is immediately healed. We may not go around healing leprosy, but Christ's touch reveals His never-ending compassion.

Christ not only healed the man physically, but he genuinely cared for him. Christ could have healed without touching the leper, but he chose to touch the unclean as if he were clean. This act would have been an affront to the religious of the day. Many times, disciples will be called upon to do that, which is not accepted by the world. Yet, because of Christ and his pure heart, we must follow his lead no matter the cost. Our eight qualities must flow through us as expressions of compassion for fellow Christians and the lost ones we encounter. These eight qualities must stem from a desire to heal spiritually and support physically the hurts and pains of those we aim to help. Compassion such as this will not come easy to the flesh. Overcoming what our eyes see demands that our faith is emboldened by a personal relationship with Christ.

Here is an example of compassion being more than a word. Travis would seek out the homeless each week and drive them to church. As Travis drove the bus, he would always pick up one gentleman who could not care for himself. As Travis loaded the man onto the bus, knowing he had been soiled for days, genuine compassion would shine. After taking everyone else to church, Travis would give this homeless man a bath and wash his clothes just in time to get back and hear the gospel. Travis was willing to touch the unclean homeless with Christ's compassion. How far are we willing to go to honor God the way He honors us? Christ's love flowing through us creates a desire to help others in ways we currently cannot imagine.

TANGIBLE IDENTIFICATION WITH CHRIST

16 Let your light so shine before men, that they may see your good works, and glorify your Father which is in heaven. Matthew 5:16

Our discipleship walk with Christ must be visible to everyone we encounter. Christ will not be hidden from the world regardless of the situation or the people we meet. Allowing others to see our Christian walk and our love for every man, woman, and child is not about claiming glory for ourselves. Glory must always be credited to the Father.

"Ye are the light of the world. A city that is set on a hill cannot be hid." Matthew 5:14

We are no longer our own. Our qualities must be visible to all and precisely identified with Christ. Being identified with Christ demands we are not ~~confused~~ entangled in the ways of the world. Our actions must show we are about our Father's business. Usually, the first statement from people that do not know Christ after our salvation is that we think we are better than them. This statement is a defense mechanism as they try to justify what they are doing when we refuse to participate. We are not to act like we are better than anyone but must stand on God's Word in all speech, actions, and interactions.

TANGIBLE VALUE OF DISCIPLESHIP

The eight qualities are tangible assets from the King of Kings. He has given us the tools to reach those who will listen and the power to speak to all, regardless of their stature. Such engagement cannot occur through our ability but instead results from the power afforded to us by the Holy Spirit through faith. There is value in loving the unlovable even when they fail to hear the truth. Speaking into people's lives as we glorify the Father regardless of their reaction is our identity in Christ and our act of discipleship.

12 Wherefore seeing we also are compassed about with so great a cloud of witnesses, let us lay aside every weight and the sin which doth so easily beset us, and let us run with patience the race that is set before us. Hebrews 12:1

The "cloud of witnesses" may include more than saints in Heaven watching our race and cheering. The cloud of witnesses may also include the lost and needy who observe as they try to understand if our faith is worth having. Let us not forget we are witnesses for Christ as soon as we profess to be Christians. The scripture's application of the plural "us" should touch the heart as it assures us that we do not run our race alone. Christ will never leave us during the race; He is ever-present.

The Eight

1. <u>Encouraging</u>: Capable of communicating God's love.
Therefore comfort each other and edify one another, just as you also are doing. 1 Thessalonians 5:11

i. "It is clear that in the primitive churches, the care of souls was not delegated to an individual officer or even the more gifted brethren among them; it was a work in which every believer might have a share." (Hiebert) [13]

2. <u>Passionate</u>: Passion that positively influences others

2 That he no longer should live the rest of his time in the flesh to the lusts of men, but to the will of God. *1 Peter 4:2*

---

[13] https://enduringword.com/bible-commentary/1-thessalonians-5/

3. <u>Inspirational</u>: Inspiring others through our daily walk

> [9] Have not I commanded thee? Be strong and of good courage; be not afraid, neither be thou dismayed: for the LORD, thy God is with thee whithersoever thou goest. *Joshua 1:9*

4. <u>Honest</u>: Integrity that inspires trust

> [3] The integrity of the upright shall guide them: but the perverseness of transgressors shall destroy them. *Proverbs 11:3*

5. <u>Empowering</u>: Work to develop others' potential

> [9] And let us not be weary in well doing: for in due season we shall reap if we faint not. *Galatians 6:9*

6. <u>Culturally Aware</u>: Flexible in all situations

> [28] There is neither Jew nor Greek, there is neither bond nor free, there is neither male nor female: for ye are all one in Christ Jesus. Galatians 3:28

7. <u>Motivational</u>: Instills a sense of purpose in others

> [10] Fear thou not; for I am with thee: be not dismayed; for I am thy God: I will strengthen thee; yea, I will help thee; yea, I will uphold thee with the right hand of my righteousness.
> *Isaiah 41:10*

8. <u>Authentic</u>: Leads through following

> [16] All scripture is given by inspiration of God, and is profitable for doctrine, for reproof, for correction, for instruction in righteousness:
>
> *2 Timothy 3:16*

Collectively, we learn to mobilize the eight assets in tangible ways, reaching people near and far. These tangible assets will bring to light the presence and effectiveness of Christ in our lives. This presence will display itself in situations where we do not even speak of Him. God's spirit is ever-present and evident through our obedience, desire, and dedication to glorifying Him in all things. Witnessing in love through word or action will transform the lives of our family members, friends, and strangers. The believer's spirit witnesses boldly as we learn to follow Christ closer.

5 Why Strive

Developing as a disciple is essential for Christians to thrive in today's environment as they prepare to face tomorrow's challenges. Understanding our call to discipleship requires that we live out the 3C's communion, community, and commission. Remembering that following God's call is why we have joy and peace throughout life's trials.

> 7 *"And the peace of God, which passeth all understanding, shall keep your hearts and minds through Christ Jesus." (Philippians 4:7)*

Such peace takes the form of God's protection. His peace is complex and defies human nature or the very essence of what we think and feel. Even the most faithful Christian fails to grasp the nuances of God's peace.

> *These things I have spoken unto you, that in me ye might have peace. In the world ye shall have tribulation: but be of good cheer; I have overcome the world. John 16:33*

As Christ conquered death, so He conquers our failings and fears, providing comfort in each believer's heart. The shedding of His righteous, untainted blood represented a gift, both precious and undeserved. The repayment of such a gift is impossible. However, the gift demands a response even if it cannot be repaid. When the answer is "I am yours Christ" and "I will serve," then we have no other choice but to "Go."

19 **Go ye, therefore**, *and teach all nations" (Matthew 28:19).*

We are not only beholden to the call of the great commission, but we also desire to serve our master and Lord by obeying His call to "Go!" The world awaits us. Those who are beaten, battered, and bruised anticipate Christ's hands and feet to be revealed through our actions. Our calling from Christ is to Go and love on His behalf.

The Unreached

Striving to be a disciple not only provides inner peace but stirs up a desire to impact the unreached for Christ's glory. Helping guide the ones the world deems unchangeable somehow becomes a comfort to the heart of the disciple. This is where the path through the narrow gate leads as we hike and climb to Heaven. Disciples not only fulfill their calling but bare their hearts along the way as they grow out of service to others. Every person, regardless of their stature in this world, desires to know about Christ and His precious gift. The ones that lash out in response to the gospel are the ones that desire to have the void filled in their hearts. That is why disciples let God be the judge of people as they deliver the good news of Christ. The unreached await us.

FAMILY

Expect friends and family will usually distance themselves from us or challenge our calling. This is the reason we must stay faithful, continue to learn, and build a testimony. Family and friends challenge our change more than anyone else as they know all our secrets and cannot believe we truly changed. Yet our Family and friends need to know the love of Christ, and they are waiting for us.

Christians will never impact our family for Christ if our Christianity is hidden behind a frail, inactive Christian walk that does not come close to victorious living. When serving a King as His emissary, the requirement is that we answer our call boldly and live out every circumstance of life while giving God glory.

What impedes us from reaching out to others when we have the one cure to each person's heart sickness? Are we uncaring? Are we selfish? In other words, what brand of faith do we claim to practice if we do not speak on Christ's behalf? Do we serve and trust Him and afford Him a top priority in our life? Remember that our family and friends await us.

FULFILLMENT AND JOY

Seeking the path of true discipleship is a life-changing event. Seeing God at work because of our obedience to "Go" becomes the most fulfilling part of our life. I implore you to take time to pray alone. Ask forgiveness for not discipling. We are not called to a singular walk with Christ, although alone time is special. We are called to each other like Christ was called to every man, woman, and child; He did not carry the sin of one person while excluding that of another. He bore the sin of the world.

Asking why to strive to be a disciple is also to ask why to keep God's grace to ourselves. I wrestled with these questions seeking answers to why I entombed the hope given to the world within my heart. The one medicine that cures all, and I have not dispensed it to the hurting. As I sought and asked, I was broken with the thought that Christians were missing out on the blessings that come with obedience. Choosing not to be bold in Christ or share the gospel to those near and far, means we risk living this life without victory. Christians miss out on God's joy when we fail to honor the word "Go." Remember, those we must reach are waiting for us.

"Comfort comes from knowing that people have made the same journey. And solace comes from understanding how others have learned to sing again."

Helen Steiner Rice

"When we are no longer able to change a situation, we are challenged to change ourselves"
Viktor E Frankl

WE MUST AS CHRISTIANS STRIVE TO
BE DISCIPLES BECAUSE A DYING
WORLD AWAITES US!

6 NEW DISCIPLE EXPECTATIONS

New disciples can expect their life's focus to change as they learn the importance of walking daily in the guidance of Christ and His Word. These lessons involve evaluation, emotion, and enlightenment. Our heart leads us to never to assume that seekers will search for us. Each Disciple Learns to Find Seekers and Value them as Christ values us.

EVALUATION

True discipleship demands that Christ's light shines brightly within the Christian heart. This light reveals what extent we love our culture and the people around us, as well as what is important to us. The process of evaluation offers a telescoped look at how each of us defines success in the absence of Christ's leadership. Such self-evaluation shifts our focus away from ourselves and temporary fulfillment, to loving others and seeking eternal satisfaction. No longer will trophies or other awards drive us to invest time, relationship, and mission. The shiny objects man bestows as awards will no longer satisfy our awakened Christian spirit. The evaluation process opens our eyes to sacrifices we have made in family time, relationships, and mission to pursue the shiny accolades that will be fruitless in eternity.

Sacrifices are still required, but new sacrifices are carried out in the service of and for Christ alone. In other words, giving of our time, talent, and testimony requires commitment. Still, it is nothing compared to all that we are promised in eternity. Indeed, our new pursuits will allow us to accumulate "trophies" of a different sort that, when we get to Heaven, we will cast at the Savior's feet. Such heavenly trophies will be the souls we helped pull from the depths of depravity and hopelessness. That is, the least, the lost, and the last will be our crown jewels and trophies that only the Father can bestow.

EMOTION

During the journey, we may feel uncomfortable when the truth reveals itself in ways that fill our hearts with dread. However, understand that we are never alone; throughout YOUR4, we are surrounded by those who are also exploring. The feelings of fear and failure fade as we embrace one another in Communion, Community, and Commission. As we learn to share life with YOUR4, we build a structure of which Christ is the cornerstone. The resultant relational community represents a place for new communities of YOUR4 disciples.

The importance we place on success must be addressed. Questions in our prayer time include: What is success to me as a Christian? Where do I put God in my life? How do I reach the least, lost, and last of these that surround me? Our answers determine Christ's priority in our hearts. The enlightenment process helps us discover the actions we are willing to take for the "Big K" Kingdom. Such steps may be as simple as sending a text to someone in need of encouragement or as complicated as sitting in a hospital. At the same time, a loved one finds their home in Heaven or God forbid, hell.

The path of discipleship is not linear. Instead, it involves surrender to God as he develops, through our obedience, the path He wants us to travel. The curvy road we have loathed in the past becomes comfortable as we learn to be obedient to the Father in all ways. Spreading the gospel and shining light within a dark world are outcomes of our obedience.

YOUR4 Discipleship calls us to journey with our Christian eyes wide open, urging us to "Go Find Them." The least, the lost, and the last are those Christ placed in our lives. Our hearts break for them. Opening our spiritual eyes to their existence and needs

> *Disciples demonstrate who Christ is & live out His longing for Every Man, Woman, & Child!*

allows us to see how we can have an eternal impact on their lives. Whether through simple actions and kind words. Sharing the love of Christ becomes part of who we are and what we do; our calling governs our approach to the world.

THE BATTLE OF DISCIPLES

Full grace is on display in the lives of Christ and the apostles. However, no one experiences full grace in the absence of a fierce battle. We fight such battles throughout our daily life because our sinful flesh calls us to live in ways that contradict the calling of Christ. When we allow full grace to conquer our hearts and minds, our decisions threaten Satan's desires for our flesh, which results in a battle.

This spiritual battle will rage within, seeking to turn aside the calling placed on our hearts. We start to understand the experience of fighting to complete "tasks" like bible reading, prayer, or speaking to those we encounter. This battle will never end no matter how many times we have victory; Satan will continue to attack. These small battles are worth the fight considering the cost of salvation, to which our hope so dearly clings.

Breaking down barriers put in place through years of gatherings and ritualistic Christianity will come at a price. Satan will stop at nothing to dissuade us from continuing. The sneak attacks are often subtle; even during this writing, Satan has worked to change or realign thoughts and words. David Platt puts it as follows:

"Radical obedience to Christ is not easy; it is dangerous. It is not smooth sailing aboard a luxury liner; it is sacrificial duty aboard a troop carrier. It's not comforts, not health, not wealth, and not prosperity in this world. Radical obedience to Christ risks losing all these things. But in the end, such risk finds its reward in Christ. And he is more than enough for us." [14]

Reread Platt's quote slowly. Ensure it sinks into our religious psyche, replacing the institutional idea of what it means to follow Christ. We must allow every thought and action to filter

---

[14] *Radical: Taking Back Your Faith from the American Dream,* Pg. 181

through the Word of God to gain proper perspective and direction.

Growing in discipleship births, a new place in the heart. A separate space within the heart desiring service to Christ. This separation is contrary to the flesh. Our flesh fears and resists heartfelt service to God.

Inaction is the devil's work in action. This fear prevents the disciple from reaching out with open hands, stretching to grasp hold of full grace. As disciples, we must force a retreat of the inaction in our Christian life and let Christ's love drive us forward in love for others. YOUR4 Discipleship enables action to help create the fullness that Christ desires to live out through us.

There have been many interesting aspects of the journey to YOUR4 Discipleship. Among the most valuable things I have learned is that the heart is conflicted when left to the single act of salvation. The longing for guidance and Christian love, birthed at salvation, is powerful when a relational ministry is encouraged and provided. Failure to lead the new Christian into discipleship within a relational community allows cheap grace to confuse the heart and mind of the young believer. This confusion manifests itself in inaction and failure to learn the deeper truths of full grace. The outcome is the denial of a true biblical community and a victorious life in Christ to the young Christian.

Creating disciples conquers conflicted hearts and allows new Christians to find community and relationships with other Christians. They are excited to learn more about God and to share what they have learned. The Christian's life, thereby, becomes exciting, and their hearts fill with joy and peace that comes directly from Christ. At this point, weekly trips to the building will no longer be enough. Disciples desire engagement with God daily.

Sacrifices to serve Christ always require struggles, but the life of reward through peace and hope will overcome all adversity.

TEACH AND LOVE

The passion for discipleship has been neglected due to the singular focus of evangelism. It is time to rekindle the desire to share life with each other bringing back into focus the calling from Christ of discipleship.

Repositioning our hearts and minds toward the complete call from Christ will ignite the gospel fire. A dual focus requires the call to "Go ye therefore and teach all nations" (evangelism) and the command to "love your neighbor as yourself" (discipleship). These callings cannot be reduced to a singular focus for the sake of simplicity or failure to invest time. We must embrace both calls as a singular purpose. The call to teach and love must be unified, as one does not exist without the other.

We are called to teach about Christ's full grace, which leads to hope. After that, we must invest in others through Christ and facilitate victorious walks through discipleship. One call without the other is a recipe for cheap grace and distorts the call placed on the new Christian's heart. A conflicted heart is not fertile terrain for the desires to teach or to love. Such desires fade beneath the pressures of life and may disappear in such conditions. In the absence of an actual gospel call and the peace that comes through obedience, the seed dies before it sees the sun.

Christ calls us to follow in His footsteps seeking all things that glorify him. The resultant journey can be summed up through the acts of glorifying, exalting, and praising God. Cheap grace involves taking salvation without changing one's path, praying without conviction, or praying without being willing to conform to Christ afterward. Such ineffective prayer creates within many Christians a false sense of security that eventually leads to hell. The person with a false sense of salvation will be the most difficult to reach. Yet by investing time and living as an example of Christ, we may be able to impact their life.

The real conversion of the man leads him to seek Christ by living a transformational life in alignment with God's Word. The narrow path leads to full grace, happiness, peace, hope, and ultimately to heaven. The body of Christ has shifted so much, that too often we accept a cheapened salvation that demands no action, no conviction, and no change of heart. This version of salvation places people in the gathering without guidance. This cannot lead to anything other than a life of frustration without victory. If the heart of a man defines him, then we must realize that without a change of heart, there can be no change of man. Conviction following salvation works within the man, as he seeks daily to conform and transform his life to be Christ-like.

True conversion changes a person's direction through sanctification and alignment with God's Word. Our willingness to align our lives with God engages us completely after conversion. The engagement process is strengthened when the body of Christ engages in the dual purposes of teaching and loving the new Christian.

Disciples of Christ will have our thinking challenged. This will leave us with unanswered questions. Obtaining the answers that we seek requires an in-depth look at our Christian walk through a biblical lens.

As we peer into the Bible for answers, we must take into consideration all aspects of a Christian's walk. We must seek to be Christ-like in all actions. One might expect such an evaluation to be straightforward, short, and to the point. However, the assessment is a continuous process during which the Christian draws closer to Christ and His control. We will never be there until we are there.

During one's self-evaluation, an understanding will emerge. That is, the Christian recognizes that all paths where Christ leads, regardless of the pain, ultimately affords a better view of our glorious savior. As we listen and learn more about the savior and His path, we see that the strait gate offers the way forward. The narrow gate is grace, and the only way through is Jesus. Understanding this narrow gate from Luke will be a revelation to our spiritual walk.

> *24 Strive to enter in at the strait gate: for many, I say unto you, will seek to enter in, and shall not be able. Luke 13:24*

The idea of gate size must be God's. In the absence of his guidance, many items, actions, or thoughts will pass through unchecked. Do not miss the word Luke uses to start the verse "strive." This word "strive" literally means to agonize. The human heart desires to hold onto the things of this world and rationalize their acceptability. Any attempt to lay aside the desires of the flesh creates agony within the man. Holding onto this world and walking in sin is easy but leads to destruction. Although, many change the outside attempting to look or act spiritually.

This type of change does not fit through the narrow gate as the strait or narrow gate requires an internal transformation. With this inner transformation, know that we will face afflictions, temptations, and persecutions yet will live in hope and arrive in Heaven at our appointed time.

As we travel through the narrow gate, we will come to understand fulfilling God's call to be a body requires a Christian relational community.

14 Now we exhort you, brethren, warn them that are unruly, comfort the feebleminded, support the weak, be patient toward all men.

1 Thessalonians 5:14

25 That there should be no schism in the body; but that the members should have the same care one for another. 26 And whether one member suffer, all the members suffer with it, or one member be honoured, all the members rejoice with it. 27 Now ye are the body of Christ, and members in particular.

1 Corinthians 12:25-27

These two verses give us direction to support one another in spiritual and physical weakness. This cannot be done if we never assemble with our brothers and sisters. "Assemble" does not only mean gathering in a building on Sunday mornings. I am using "assemble" here to say coffee together and sharing one another's burdens. To live out a relational community will require that we invest in one another to the point that we can trust each other with our problems.

Trusting one another will eventually create a community where we support and love spiritually, allowing the secrets of the heart to be dragged into the light. These secrets may not be earth-shattering, but they affect our spiritual wellbeing and need to be dealt with together. Secrets such as gossip, lying, porn, or even unclean thoughts that we struggle to control. The idea of who I am, deep down, makes me cringe as I stand at the narrow gate. But we must remember Satan does not want us to find help for our hurts or hands for our support. Satan desires that we follow our hearts. Yet as Christians, we know this to be a dangerous path. Our hearts are wicked without Christ and deceitful even to the man that thinks he has everything under God's hand. We may think we know our hearts, but we must not be fooled. As Jeremiah 17 states:

> *9The heart is deceitful above all things, and desperately wicked: who can know it? 10I the LORD searches the heart, I try the reins, even to give every man according to his ways, and according to the fruit of his doings. (Jeremiah 17:9-10)*

Learning to lean on God and allowing Him to guide our hearts will expose each speck of sin that must be removed. Our community will help through support, prayer, and study of God's Word. As prideful and self-interested hearts surfaces, we must learn to deal with it as a body. In dealing with our shared pains and shortcomings, our community and the body of Christ will be strengthened. The difference between the lost and saved is that the saved have a supporting relational community and never suffer alone.

As disciples, we continually deal with the smallest speck in the heart until total surrender is accomplished. This surrender requires us to lean into God's grasp and ultimately leads to our spiritual healing. Each step we take toward Christ through service and sacrifice results in the satisfaction of our hearts. The type of satisfaction non-serving Christians can only imagine. We become alive in who Christ is and consider service to the King a privilege, not an obligation.

Throughout our Hiking and Climbing Journey, we learned to let God's shining light pierce our human understanding and replace it with His truth. Thereby desiring to draw closer to Christ each day regardless of cost. Focusing on who we are as Christians and how we live out our faith is essential to understanding our journey with God. Looking back, we will be excited about what God has done, is doing, and what he has planned. As we continue to follow God and allow his thoughts to permeate every aspect of who we are the narrow gate will continue to shrink allowing us to squeeze through as the world is forced to let go.

7 LEADERSHIP TOOLS

What's in it for me?

None of us want to spend our valuable time doing something that does not move us forward. That is why there are questions to answer when considering our activities: What is in it for me? What is required? What do I need to get started?

What is in it for me? As Christians, we must aim to adopt a biblically correct walk, a heart for the broken, life-changing relationships, and love for the community. As we undertake discipleship, we must grasp that moving from self-focus to a focus on relational community repositions our hearts, allowing a closer alignment with Christ. It is no longer enough to be satisfied living an independent life of self-service. Our desires must align with Jesus, and then our willingness to live in a missional community with others will come to life. It should also be noted that a genuine call to discipleship (salvation) removes the "What is in it for me" question. Our focus should be on how to glorify Christ through action. That has been pointed out through being sent as Christ was sent in John 20:21. We are to deny ourselves and take up our cross daily.

WHAT'S REQUIRED?

Each step in the journey leads to one body in Christ. Completing YOUR4 Discipleship involves daily bible reading, daily prayer, biweekly group meetings, and open discussions and actions, facilitating growth and spiritual development. Such tasks require space in our life if we are to live victoriously as the King's child. Christians know these activities are the foundation, yet we omit them from our schedules, our lives, and therefore impair our chances at victory. YOUR4 Hiking should have developed within our hearts a desire to spend time with God and others. Moving forward, if communion with God, community with others, or commission to our culture starts to fade, then we have probably gone back to facing the world alone. The second "C"- community cannot fall to the back as it is the pillar on earth that holds us true and steady. Loving God and loving others are two interconnected pillars. We cannot indeed have one without the other. Understand what we have learned through the YOUR4 journey. God is love, and once we love God, we learn to love others as ourselves. We must not delude ourselves into thinking that our love for God is a personal thing not to be shared. Jesus walked the earth with a heart for all people, not just a love for the Father, and we are to follow His model.

12And though a man might prevail against one who is alone, two will withstand him a threefold cord is not quickly broken. Ecclesiastes 4:12

WHAT DO I NEED?

A broken and contrite heart desires growth and blessing. YOUR4 Discipleship is about seeking a deeper relationship with God and others, thereby soothing the inward desire to be one in Christ's Body. For relationships to blossom, we must learn to put ourselves aside, placing others at the front. I encourage you to read the Psalm below multiple times, allowing it to bind God into your heart. Look to Him for mercy and direction. He holds both and desires to give freely.

"This great song, pulsating with the agony of a sin-stricken soul, helps us to understand the stupendous wonder of the everlasting mercy of our God." (G. Campbell Morgan)

Have mercy on me,[a]O God, according to your steadfast love, according to your abundant mercy blot out my transgressions. 2 Wash me thoroughly from my iniquity and cleanse me from my sin! 3 For I know my transgressions, and my sin is ever before me. 4 Against you, you only, have I sinned and done what is evil in your sight so that you may be justified in your words and blameless in your judgment 5 Behold, I was brought forth in iniquity, and in sin, did my mother conceive me. 6 Behold, you delight in truth in the inward being, and you teach me wisdom in the secret heart. 7 Purge me with hyssop, and I shall be clean; wash me, and I shall be whiter than snow. 8 Let me hear joy and gladness; let the bones that you have broken rejoice. 9 Hide your face from my sins and blot out all my iniquities. 10 Create in me a clean heart, O God, and renew a right[b] spirit within me. 11 Cast

me not away from your presence and take not your Holy Spirit from me. ¹² Restore to me the joy of your salvation and uphold me with a willing spirit. ¹³ Then I will teach transgressors your ways, and sinners will return to you. ¹⁴ Deliver me from bloodguiltiness, O God, O God of my salvation, and my tongue will sing aloud of your righteousness. ¹⁵ O Lord open my lips, and my mouth will declare your praise. ¹⁶ For you will not delight in sacrifice, or I would give it; you will not be pleased with a burnt offering. ¹⁷ The sacrifices of God are a broken spirit; a broken and contrite heart, O God, you will not despise.
(Psalm 51:1-17)

Where is God?

The Priority Circle and Time Study were our first steps. There are three Priority Circles and three Time Studies in the YOUR4 curriculum. Once we completed YOUR4 Hiking, we should have placed each set side by side. Assessing any patterns that emerge reveals the trajectory of our growth throughout the YOUR4 process. The assessment may also reveal areas in which further growth is in order.

Noting areas in which we have opportunities to grow, positions us to tap into the relational community as a support network. Involvement in a relational community offers a structure of accountability to Christ and His gospel through the body of Christ. In the absence of an accountability system, everyone is at risk of falling prey to the enemy's attacks. Remember Jeremiah 17:9-10; our hearts are deceitful. At times, we need someone to hold the light for us so we can see where we are headed.

S.O.A.P – What Next?

S.O.A.P. entries were conducted six days a week. The seventh day is for Life Together or your church service. As we completed the daily S.O.A.P.S, we have noticed one- or two-word critical concepts from the verses. Now that we have completed the twelve-week program, review all notes. Create a list of key concepts from each day of each week. The list should reveal the path traveled to discipleship. An example is found below from lesson one.

<u>Salvation leads to</u> Surrender, learning about God, Concern for Others, Understanding God is First, Being Like Christ, and Filtering Life.

The six verses from which we drew the key concepts, provided a roadmap after we accepted Christ. The use of crucial concepts ought to be employed for the remaining S.O.A.P. verses in YOUR4 Hiking. As we work our way through the steps, notice that everything in life, including actions, activities, and desires, must be filtered through the Word, and thereby cleansed. In Week One, we traversed the trail of exploration as we learned about the steps that follow Salvation.

S.O.A.P – Will I need Them?

Many participants consider the written sheets the most challenging component of the program. As we review each week, however, we notice a complete teacher's manual has been created for use in our next YOUR4. Having written the manual ourselves, we will feel fully in command of how to lead our first YOUR4 session. The time we spent composing the written work was time well spent. As we are teaching a session, our notes will keep us grounded and boost our confidence as we step out in response to what God has called us to do.

Throughout leading our first YOUR4, re-S.O.A.P. the verses keeping another set of notes as well. Investing in another set of notes is valuable because God consistently reveals new information if we are attuned to what he is offering and diligent in seeking. Through leading, we will participate in another round of priority circles and time studies. Continue to evaluate time and priorities as you seek to draw closer to God.

Habits – Seeking God First.: During YOUR4 Hiking, we will have developed a daily rhythm such as bible reading, praying, sharing, and evaluating our hearts and lives. After twelve weeks, this rhythm will prove to be invaluable in our efforts to glorify God each day. Firmly ingrained rhythms or habits will consistently drive us to remain mindful of our commitment to God and loving others.

Actions – Boldness in Christ: It may have seemed ridiculous to text or call people in our group. However, those small actions were baby steps that prepared us to feel comfortable reaching out to others. The coffee talks engaged each person in sharing life with others. Such experiences and practices are valuable because of the extent to which we tend to behave in self-serving ways instead of reaching out to offer or receive help. Breaking free of a selfish mindset by engaging with other people in relational ministry is the essence of being part of the body of Christ.

For example, praying out loud at coffee talk taught us that prayer to the savior is an honor as opposed to an action that should create fear. Satan desires us to believe people are watching and judging to prevent our bold witness before others. The simple act of praying aloud can conquer the self-doubt increasing confidence in our spiritual ability. The simple act of praying aloud in some small way crucifies the flesh, and with each small step, we grow to be warriors in all circumstances for the gospel. Taking each little action draws us closer to Christ and crushes the enemy.

> *37 Nay, in all these things we are more than conquerors through him that loved us. Romans 8:37*

Christ provides the strength to conquer the small and large issues of life when we trust Him. We cannot say we trust Christ and His Word yet fail to speak on His behalf. If we decide we are not going to speak up for Christ because of fear, how do we reconcile 2 Timothy with our faith?

> *7 for God gave us a spirit not of fear but of power and love and self-control. 2 Timothy 1:7*

Through the love of God, we have an infinite power to overcome fear in all circumstances. I use the small act of praying out loud as an example. I have experienced many that will not speak one word for God and thereby fail to master the broader circumstances of life. Mastering the small things will lead us to conquer the giants that lurk in the darkness.

Given the access we have to the scriptures and the throne room of glory through prayer, how do we fail to stand bold in Christ? What happens when it is not a simple public prayer but real persecution? Serving an almighty God demands we follow His leading and His direction. The uncomfortableness of praying out loud, witnessing, or serving in any capacity can be overcome through the gospel. We must remember that the gospel is not a friend to the flesh. The gospel calls us to be Christlike or the opposite of our lost nature. The importance of serving in all aspects cannot be stressed enough as the battles will gain momentum and size.

As we continue our journey, it becomes apparent that nothing can span the chasm of faith or lack thereof. We either serve Christ with all that we are as our master, or we do not. Serving Christ costs the flesh but only temporarily. It is not possible to move back and forth between serving Christ and not serving Christ. This is not to say we do not fall or sin, but it points to the heart. As Ephesians 2:8-9 states, we are saved by grace and not of ourselves. When truly saved, we will desire to follow God and feel remorse when we fail Him. The Christian's heart always places Christ at the forefront, no matter the situation, challenge, or small prayer to be spoken.

GROWING TOGETHER

Coffee talks started as places to review and discuss the S.O.A.P. findings. They were also designed for people to begin developing a Christian community. Over time, the emphasis on S.O.A.P. talks should have shifted toward a more organically defined time of fellowship with our missional community. Coffee talks are opportunities to reach into each other's lives and help through listening and prayer. Coffee talks whether with a YOUR4 group or someone we are meeting for the first time should be viewed as strategic. These talks are to be prepared through prayer. Coffee talks can be utilized to intentionally help shoulder one another's burdens. As this begins to take place, the family of God, or better yet, the pure body of Christ, will be revealed. We should have caught the hint by now that I value the coffee talk, breakfast talk, or dinner talk. Any time we can meet with someone to witness and share life together, it is a win for the Kingdom. What initially may seem like insignificant meetings are investments that lead people to Christ. Since I believe so much in the coffee talk, below are a few ideas when we get together with small groups to break the ice

WHY COFFEE TALK?

Bringing people together: to harmonize relationships, talk about important topics, build trust relationships. Coffee Talk can get you there.

<u>Prepare</u>

1. Think about who should attend (everyone or individual).

2. Brainstorm about their common topics, purposes.

3. Pray for each one.

4. Discuss questions from S.O.A.P. Chit chat, General Conversation.

> Advantages: Generates trust, Gain insights into their faith, Strengthen bonds, Small investment for large reward – Connections

<u>Touch of Inspiration</u>

1. Thank God He chose you to lead His children

2. Goal: Bring people closer together, fostering relationships across multiple life experiences.

Start with icebreaker questions

1. If you could choose to be one age forever, what age would that be, and why?

2. Follow Main Topic: Discuss the multiple S.O.A.P. cards brought. You can discuss one or many. You Decide!

3. If needed, switch between icebreaker-topics: What are the three most important items you own?

<u>Make Coffee Talks Inspirational:</u> Coffee talks will become a big part of your YOUR4 life. Many options skype, zoom, face time, preferably in person, etc. How can we make the most of these opportunities?

10 Steps to an Inspirational Coffee Talk

(ASK YOURSELF)

1. Do we need this meeting?

2. What is its purpose?

3. Who needs to attend?

HOST/HOSTESS WITH THE MOSTEST:

5. Make everyone comfortable take a few minutes for chit-chat

6. Start and end on time. Note: Ending on time does not mean everyone has to leave. This only indicates the facilitated time is complete. Usually, people stay for hours after the meeting. These after-hours are where real ministry takes place. This also shows the hunger for compassion and real conversation.

7. Listen. Stay open and engaged.

8. Share the mic - Let others speak.

9. Encourage participation but do not force.

NEVER LOSE SIGHT:

10. End coffee time with positivity & encouragement to continue the journey God has set before each of us. It is okay if everyone walks away with a few items to work on before the next meeting.

<u>Add some fun</u>

1. Get comfortable with some fun questions: What is your favorite movie, and why?
2. Start at an unusual time.
3. Make it a talk show and not a one-person show.
4. Switch seats during the meeting.
5. Never be afraid to insert an icebreaker.

<u>Coffee with a Twist:</u> In this big world, it is more and more difficult connecting with people, even those sitting next door. YOUR4 has answers!

WHAT IS COFFEE TALK?

Urban dictionary: talking and rehashing the **ups** and downs of life, while sipping **coffee**, which increases the importance and maturity of all those involved

Miscellaneous Forms –

Heart Evaluations

Filling in the forms about who we texted or what S.O.A.P. we took to coffee talk is an opportunity to reflect on what makes us tick and why. If we seek to understand better our actions with Christ in mind as a model, it will hasten our progress down the path of discipleship. That is, we behave one way or another for a reason. Identifying and reflecting on that reason points us in a direction of growth. For instance, we may discover a personal bias of which we were unaware. Regular assessment of our heart's intent and desire considering God's Word is integral to the journey of a disciple.

How can I help?

This card was in the YOUR4 program to invite each one to reach out to our leaders for assistance. Our journeys are collective experiences. No one travels alone. Issues that we need to address will be among matters others have on their lists as well. Identifying areas for growth we have in common will make reaching more comfortable because we have a starting place for relationship building.

YOUR4 Their Journey –

Building Relationships

In week six, we filled in the YOUR4 card identifying people we interact with and who we might lead through YOUR4 Hiking. After identifying those people, we texted and called them. The objective was to engage in the process of building relationships. Telling someone we are praying for them once does not build the spiritual capital required to lead them in a walk with Christ. However, regular contact creates clout because it establishes a sense of our continued investment, which displays the love of Christ. If we shine the gospel light into a person's eyes, it blinds them for a minute. They will tend to close their eyes or turn away. Yet, if we continue to shine light into the darkness, the person's eyes will adjust to the new condition. They will see what they never knew existed, mainly the love of Christ. The urge to turn away will fade and give way to a desire to turn toward Christ. Therefore, our work represents an ongoing commitment to shining God's light of hope repeatedly into the darkness. Exposing the reality up to this point, was unseen.

8 WEEKS IN REVIEW

As we review the method, we likely recognize the objective for each of its components. Hiking equipped us to spread the gospel to create disciples of Christ. It does not matter where we are in our walk with Christ; everyone is called to be a disciple. If we are newly saved, then we know what God changed in our life. Thus, we can witness about our experience better than anyone else. We know how to pray because we prayed for salvation. Invite someone to share something for which they would like you to pray on their behalf and do it. God honors those who honor Him through acts of service.

Christians who are further along on their journeys must bear in mind that new converts have much to learn. Thus, more "advanced" Christians need to bring babes in Christ along without belittling or judging them for what they have yet to learn. Embrace each small step new Christians take, and celebrate their Hiking journey.

WEEKS 1-4 BASICS OF COMMUNION

Weeks one through four took a deeper dive into Communion with God through understanding Salvation, Baptism, Bible Study, and Prayer life. A new understanding of where we stand will propel us forward in seeking the tenets of God's full grace in our lives and reaching out in Christ's name with love and compassion. The fogginess that clouded our mind and heart in the past will burn away through the light of understanding. As the fogginess dissipates, and the light shines brighter, we learn to embrace God and His calling. We realize that our hearts and minds are infiltrated with a desire, or better yet, placed on mission, to reach the least, the lost, and the last of mankind.

An enriched understanding of God's Word and opportunities to commune with Him during the first four weeks should have sparked a fire within us to, "Go ye therefore." New callings and ideas now burst forth from the heart with an urgency we likely have never experienced. The urgency of the call and the need to comfort the hurting will continue to intensify through our daily walk. The single call to people will give birth to many avenues for fulfilling this call. Seeking God's guidance and living out the Great Commission will transform our Christian walk into something more powerful than we can comprehend. Therefore, we must allow our yearnings to move us forward in our communion with God, always loving others as we love ourselves.

WEEK 5 BASICS OF COMMUNITY

Week five focused on seeking Community with others and on Christ's call to relational ministry within the big "K" Kingdom. Community excitement likely built in the preceding four weeks. Week five exposes us to the importance of believers or the body of Christ, and how participating in sharing relational ministry grows us together and glorifies God. Our S.O.A.P. verses have enabled us to see how God expects us to interact with others. Often, we attend a gathering and call it church. After returning home, we face life alone, finding ourselves hurting with no sense of direction out of the pain. Is this what God desires? Does God want us to suffer alone outside of the body of Christ? Surely, he does not, one part of the body cannot hurt without the other parts, also experiencing pain. The finger cannot hurt apart from the hand, and neither should we hurt apart from the Body. If we are hurting alone, both our isolation and our pain require remedy. Otherwise, attacks by the enemy will escalate. We need to learn to garner the support of the army.

Spending time together and trusting one another allows us to deepen our Christian relationships together. Often, we forget our fellow brothers and sisters, even though the Word reminds us. The institutional church gathers people into one place. Yet, we seem to have lost the care and support of life together outside of the building. Supporting and loving one another leads to our communities fostering spiritual growth, hope, and comfort in Christ. Sacrificially loving others as Christ loved us is what each disciple is called to do.

WEEK 6 SHARING JESUS

COMMISSION

Week six offers an exciting time of discovery as we begin to better understand our path to laying crowns before the Savior's feet. In Week 6, we filled in our YOUR4 Their Journey card. The names of those we prayed for over the preceding five weeks becomes visible to all as they are shared. This allows the community to unite their focus on praying for the next layer of disciples. YOUR4 Group can now be part of supporting our desire to invest relational capital into those with whom we communicate regularly.

God has placed people in our lives for us to lead on the path of discipleship. Remember, we all seek the least, the last, and the lost to lead to a relationship with Christ and his church. Through our leadership, we build community and relationships to share life together, no matter the circumstance.

WEEK 7 TRUSTING JESUS

During the first five weeks, we sought to draw closer to Christ and understand what His desires mean for our life. We reflected on our hearts seeking to reveal priorities concerning discipleship. Week 6, we went on a quest to reach others for Christ. Ultimately, we removed the veil covering our spiritual eyes to understand Christian interaction with those we regularly communicate. The revelation of our spiritual blindness enlightened us to what extent we are to spread Christ's love to others.

Week 7 discipleship concerns the path that guides us toward understanding how to trust Christ with our lives. Such trust involves problems, celebrations, heartache, and our material items. As our journey progresses, we must continue to expand our obedience to God's Word, through seeking His direction. Deeper prayer and bible study will be essential as we learn to place our trust in Christ as our Father and King.

Often, we attempt to shield God from many of our private desires and material idols. How odd that we believe we can hide from God. It is as though we imagine secret places that are not for God's viewing or meddling. In this hiding place, we are exhibiting a failure to trust in God with our worldly treasures while professing trust in God for our eternal state. Trusting God with our eternity should remove our hold on materialism and encourage a total surrender to our spiritual walk. Yet, many times we try and hide these sacred items to retain control. The scope of our surrender could exclude money, time, schedules, porn, screen time, and so on. Such compartmentalization, however, only points to the state of our heart.

Christ desires all of who we are, just as we wanted all His grace at salvation. He is the light of our life and, therefore, must be involved in our decisions and have access to every dark closet. What if Christ only gave us a few months in Heaven or only forgave some sin. Would we be satisfied? In the same way, when we try to serve two masters, Christ is not satisfied. Our God is jealous and will not compete with anyone or anything in our life for first place. Speaking honestly to Christ, we confess who we are to Him in all respects. Inviting God to talk freely with us, and through us, our battle cry must be "Christ is Leading Me." Success in discipleship is the outcome of obedience to God.

Six common areas of life typically held separate from God were revealed in week seven. These six common areas are released only to be reclaimed a short time later. We take all six to the altar of God only to pick them up as we complete our prayer. These secret places are where we covet control. We lock them away in our heart and refrain from giving anyone, even God, open access. True discipleship does not allow hidden areas as we work on our personal relationship with God. Painful as that may sound, the surrender of our entire life brings relief, not pain. That is, turning ourselves fully over to Him allows His spirit to provide peace, repair marriages, solve money troubles, and generally take the load from our shoulders. With Christ in control, our life will be reordered into a picture of grace and light. Altering our lives on earth alters not only our eternity but also the lives of those who know us today.

We will never be fully victorious unless we surrender all things. After all, Christ gave everything for us. God does not work around our desires. Instead, He asks that we find delight in living our lives in ways that compare with His. Only then will we recognize the daily miracles performed on our behalf?

The six focus areas from week seven will reveal our heart's true surrender or lack thereof. For example, for years, I claimed, "I do not have time" for prayer or bible study. However, that was a lie. I have as much time as anyone else; how I choose to spend my time directly reflects my priorities. Ask yourself regularly, is God first in my life? Do I set aside and give God time?

Six Difficult Focus Areas

<u>Time</u>

Have you ever stopped and thought about time? That is, have you seriously delved into how you conceptualize time or think about time? When we claim not to have enough time, what do we really mean? Do we mean that we have run out of time? Have we filled our lives with activities and obligations until there is no room left for anything else? If we view time through the world's lens, an image of Father Time may come to mind. You are probably familiar with the image of the old, white, bearded man with the scythe, standing guard, and ready to take us at any moment.

Suppose that, instead of accepting the world's personification of time, we pictured Father Time as an athletic figure wearing running shoes and a ski mask. Such a depiction seems more in line with how time operates in many of our lives. Time is a thief; it steals precious moments, memories, and abilities as we march toward eternity. On earth, time today is finite, measured by the movement of hands on a clock, numbers on a dial, or the years between birth and death. In contrast, God's time is eternal. God's time is unfettered and cannot be shackled to a clock or forced to fit the confines of a calendar page. God's time is immeasurable. Committing ourselves to go full throttle toward God's unbound time ought to clarify our perspective about how we use our currently limited time.

When we were born, God created a "time account" in our names. An initial deposit of minutes is made, and the account is signed over to us, free and clear. The only stipulation is that no further deposits can be made. Only withdrawals are allowed. God gave us complete control to use our time as we see fit throughout life. He requires nothing in exchange for His gift of time, even though He desires every minute through His love. The statement "I don't have time" is not accurate for any of us. Each of us has an account and a balance. It is not that we lack time. Rather, we lack a commitment to making God a priority. We choose how to use our time. We are in control of how we spend it, whether we use it to watch television, play sports, hunt, fish, or any other activity. God, the giver, becomes last in line for our attention. Oh wait, we do give Him one hour a week at church (maybe) that should be enough.

When Christ was born in the manger, God set up His time account also. Jesus chose to spend from his account on serving us, loving us, and dying for us. Within His serving, loving, and dying, Jesus was glorifying and obeying God. We, too, need to plan how we intend to use our time on our Christian walk. Intentionality, when planning our priorities, pays dividends to our heart and soul.

Once our account is depleted, we face eternity or countless time. At that moment, we will see what survived our Earthly stay. Our legacies on Earth do not survive. The material things we have amassed will fade away. Those that remember how great a guy we were will die, taking with them the stories and memories of us. After our finite time has expired and endless time becomes a reality, the only legacy remaining is the souls we took part in leading and developing for Christ. Our legacies are comprised of crowns we will lay at the feet of the Master.

> [12] *Blessed is the man that endureth temptation: for when he is tried, he shall receive the crown of life, which the Lord hath promised to them that love him. James 1:12*

¹⁰ The four and twenty elders fall down before him that sat on the throne, and worship him that liveth for ever and ever, and cast their crowns before the throne, saying, Revelation 4:10

⁵See then that ye walk circumspectly, not as fools, but as wise, ¹⁶Redeeming the time, because the days are evil. ¹⁷Wherefore be ye not unwise but understanding what the will of the Lord is. Ephesians 5:15-16

Ephesians 16 reminds us that each day our lives are opened for new service to God. Unique opportunity abounds to spread the message of love and hope. We must take advantage of each moment as the days approach when witness and service here on earth will end. The ones that had the opportunity will no longer hear the cry of the witness to Christ. It is our finite time that we must take advantage of for the lost. Redeem each moment to pull those you love from the grasp of hell.

¹⁰ As we have therefore opportunity, let us do good unto all men, especially unto them who are of the household of faith. Galatians 6:10

What choices will we make regarding the use of time? Will we lie to God and ourselves by claiming not to have time? Are we bold enough to tell God that we will not use any of the time He gave us to serve Him? True discipleship will call us to seek God's will and do what it takes to seek His people.

"Time is a cruel thief to rob us of our former selves. We lose as much to life as we do to death."

Elizabeth Forsythe Hailey

"Time is free, but it's priceless. You cannot own it, but you can use it. You cannot keep it, but you can spend it. Once you have lost it, you can never get it back." Harvey Mackay

<u>Talent</u>

[17] And whatever you do, in word or deed, do everything in the name of the Lord Jesus, giving thanks to God the Father through him. Colossians 3:17

How do we approach Colossians 3:17? Do we apply this in daily life to conversations, youth sports, or work? Colossians does not allow any room for an interpretation that gives us an out. The "whatsoever" is a comprehensive reference to our lives. Let every action and reaction be for the glory of God. Surviving tough times requires dependence on God in strength and spirit and allows God to guide and comfort us as He desires.

Christ has given each person a gift that is special to our makeup as a person. This gift can be claimed through salvation and obedience. Christ has placed within us something unique that service to Him will unlock. This unlocking allows us to serve Him in ways more significant than we ever thought possible. At times, God's gifts get overlooked by the world and fail to attract praise and attention, which some people desire. We must remember service to God places crowns into the unfettered time of eternity, rendering unimportant the fleeting praise of this world.

[10]As each has received a gift, use it to serve one another, as good stewards of God's varied grace: 1 Peter 4:10

Testimony

¹⁹ Or do you not know that your body is a temple of the Holy Spirit within you, whom you have from God? You are not your own, ²⁰ for you were bought with a price. So, glorify God in your body. 1 Corinthians 6:19-20

Knowing that we walk with the Holy Spirit within, do we pause to contemplate how our goings may grieve the Spirit? Our bodies are temples of Christ, and we need to treat them as such. We are not our own. Do we seek God regarding actions or decisions for His temple?

Accepting that our bodies belong to Christ requires that we use them for God's glory. We should abstain from situations and actions that harm us physically, mentally, or emotionally. Aligning with Christ's Word causes some to resist and revert to old habits and reject the notion that we must use our bodies for purposes that glorify God. However, as Christians, we should desire what God desires and bring that under the control of our bodies and actions. Controlling our bodies and actions builds testimonies that go before us pave the way for outreach.

Harry Ironside was correct when he wrote, "Glorify God in your body, and the spiritual side will take care of itself."

Treasure

² On the first day of every week, each of you is to put something aside and store it up, as he may prosper so that there will be no collecting when I come. 1 Corinthians 16:2

Herein lies a stumbling block for many Christians, young and old. We are to give ourselves to God's work and the furtherance of the gospel. Engaging in gospel mission requires the body of Christ to work together in all things, including giving monetarily and physically. That is, giving is a consistent requirement that we will understand further as we seek guidance through prayer and Bible time. There should never be a man who persuades us to give but rather a movement of God in our hearts. God must direct us in all things.

> *²⁴ One gives freely yet grows all the richer; another withholds what he should give, and only suffers want. Proverbs 11:24*

I challenge you to reread the above Proverb and discuss it with YOUR4 group about the many facets of growing richer through obedience. As we discuss it, remember that we are called to live within God's will, and will be rich in ways man cannot understand. The eyes of the saint are stayed on God. Rich to a saint may not even involve this world.

<u>Tameness</u>

> *²⁹ But Peter and the apostles answered, "We must obey God rather than men. Acts 5:29*

How do you determine your reaction to situations? Do you base it on who is watching? Do you react differently in church than you do at work? These are among the questions that we must consider and for which we need to seek answers. Calming the heart is one of the most challenging tasks next to controlling the tongue. Both the calming and the control come from the heart.

18 But what comes out of the mouth proceeds from the heart, and this defiles a person. 19 For out of the heart come evil thoughts, murder, adultery, sexual immorality, theft, false witness, slander. 20 These are what defile a person. But to eat with unwashed hands does not defile anyone." Matthew 15:18-20

The tameness of the heart cannot be accomplished by man alone. Tameness comes from spending time in the Word seeking how we can become more like Jesus. Such growth comes at a price to the flesh. The selfish flesh hates the thought of being under the yoke of Christ and will fight such constraint every step of the way. I focus on what God is teaching me instead of on what He is teaching someone else. If I focus on another person, they control the situation, and the circumstances become about them instead of about how best to glorify God. But if I look to God, he can use every situation as an opportunity. Growth may emerge as patience, service, or breaking of pride. Each step takes us closer to being Christlike. Christians are called to set their heart on Christ and to follow His lead.

Tenderness

13 You will seek me and find me when you seek me with all your heart. Jeremiah 29:13

The sixth focus area is tenderness. Seeking God with a pure heart will lead us to God. God does not hide from us. Christ is available when we seek Him with a pure heart that gives Him all and glorifies Him in all. Such forms of giving are contained within the six areas of focus: time, talent, testimony, treasure, tameness, and tenderness. Submitting these six areas to Christ creates within us a tender heart toward those we encounter, just as Jesus' heart was tender. Submission or retention of these areas will shape our testimony either into glorifying God or the world. Our obedience will not be burdensome to our spirits though it will wreak havoc on the flesh. Obedience allows us to control the sinfulness of the flesh, which becomes an internal battle.

We do not regret obedience when we become disciples. The yoke of Christ is easy, and the burden is light and pleasurable. Christ wants what is His; that is us and all that we are. He wants us to allow Him to supply all that we need.

These seven weeks prepared the foundation of a disciple's identity and response to God's calling. YOUR4 Hiking is the starting point from which we reach further for the gospel kingdom.

Mt. Convergence to Mt. Trivergence

After acquiring a basic understanding of our hearts and how we approach Christ, we moved into Hiking Mt. Trivergence. This hiking experience teaches us to be the guide and lead others into discipleship. Mt Trivergence moves us away from learning about ourselves and includes others as we journey forward.

WEEK 8 FOLLOW ME

COMMUNION

The call to follow lays the groundwork for who we are in our calling. God's calling to us resembles that of a Father to a child. He calls not only out of love for the child but to protect their steps as well. God the Father desires that we follow Him, staying within His shadow of protection. His protection does not prevent life from happening, but rather it gets us through life with hope and peace that we cannot understand. By following, we learn Jesus' method of reaching people and discover how he pulls them from the grasp of sin and despair. Following in obedience shows us how Jesus loves people here on Earth. We learn to direct others out of a hopeless life. Our lessons from Christ are understood and applied when we follow closely. Seeking to emulate Christ in all we do or say, while seeking the least, the lost, and the last of this world is the work that disciples are called upon to embrace.

19 And he said to them, "Follow me, and I will make you fishers of men." Matthew 4:19

Following Christ closely represents obedience to His call. He calls us to reach people with His authority in our hands. Christ's call is personal. He sends it directly to everyone that submits to His will that is: *"I will make you fishers of men."* This statement does not say we will be on our own. Instead, it says that Jesus will transform us if we agree to follow Him.

20 Immediately they left their nets and followed him. Matthew 4:20

22 Immediately they left the boat and their father and followed him. Matthew 4:22

Following God requires us to leave things of this world behind. Some may see that as a sacrifice. I disagree. Following Christ, we always result in gaining more than we could ever give. These men left goods, nets, and boats as well as family to follow Christ. When leaving, keep your eye on the gaining that occurred because thousands were snatched from the depths of hell. The birthing of God's church on Earth and the community that supports and withstands the evil darts of Satan. What is left behind is not a sacrifice; it is a launching pad to greater things than we can imagine. As fishers of men, we function in many realms. Mission fields take many forms. Our life is a mission field. We are disciples, no matter where we stand.

WEEK 9 LIFE TOGETHER CAMPFIRE

COMMUNITY

Week nine approached the truth that we are called to engage with others in our culture. Life together is not a decision we make but something we accomplish by being one Body in Christ. God's authority becomes part of who we are in this life as we seek the next. Life together enables us to work as one in the body of Christ as we learn to love the culture outside our front door. Week nine expanded our understanding of why we need to love every man, woman, and child. The core concept of discipleship relegates any prejudices to the old man as we walk anew in Christ.

Week nine encouraged us to ask questions of what we have been taught and filter these sacred walls or worldly rituals through the Word of God. A few of these could be: Why has the call to one Body disappeared? Have the gatekeepers of Christianity allowed large gatherings to snuff out relational communities? These two can coexist, by the way. Existing as one body requires breaking down the walls of thought and religion and replacing it with God's will and direction. During Week nine, we learned that all Christians are part of the Body. This Body includes small groups, large churches, relational ministry groups, and missional ministries. I have discovered through study, that all gatherings that glorify God and follow Jesus are part of the body of Christ and should be treated as such.

There should not be competition between different movements if they are comprised of believers of the gospel of Christ, namely His death, burial, and resurrection. Being on staff at a large gathering does not make one person more of a Christ-follower than another. We are called to reach across all divides and to pull everyone in the body of Christ together. If there is competition, it is not God's doing; we should not accept the idea that any group of believers is better than another. The only competition the body of Christ should be involved in is a united battle against Satan and his forces. Let us all live in Christ through life together.

12 "For just as the body is one and has many members, and all the members of the body, though many, are one body, so it is with Christ. 13 For in one Spirit, we were all baptized into one body — Jews or Greeks, slaves[a] or free — and all were made to drink of one Spirit. 14 For the body does not consist of one member but of many." (1 Corinthians 12:12-14)

22 "On the contrary, the parts of the body that seem to be weaker are indispensable, 23 and on those parts of the body that we think less honorable we bestow the greater honor, and our unpresentable parts are treated with greater modesty, 24 which our more presentable parts do not require. But God has so composed the body, giving greater honor to the part that lacked it, 25 that there may be no division in the body, but that the members may have the same care for one another. 26 If one member suffers, all suffer together; if one member is honored, all rejoice together. 27 Now you are the body of Christ and individually members of it." (1 Corinthians 12:12-27)

WEEK 10 CULTURE AROUND US THE FUTURE

COMMISSION

Week ten focused on learning to embrace the culture around us, no matter our location. It seems appropriate that we end with the commission that leads us into the future. Reaching those around us with the gospel is an honor that ought to fill our hearts with joy. Throughout the past ten weeks, we have been learning to reach and preparing to teach. If we only reach people in the name of Christ but then leave them to their own devices, what are the odds of a victorious life? Christ placed us here as His beacon to a dying world. He called us not only to give light but to help the light stay lit in those that receive Him. The verses below didn't stop at "Go" but continued saying "teach." We are to build relationships that allow honesty when speaking into the lives of others.

> *[19]"Go therefore and make disciples of all nations, baptizing them in the name of the Father and of the Son and of the Holy Spirit, [20] teaching them to observe all that I have commanded you. And behold, I am with you always, to the end of the age." (Matthew 28:19-20)*

YOUR4 Hiking asks us to be bold in our faith yet humble in our approach. The empty toolbox we once carried in and out of service should now contain the tools required for service. Matthew 28:19-20 does not say go out if we are a theologian or preacher; it only says, "Go." We are called to be a disciple and sharer of the gospel. We are to share it with those we encounter on the mission field, whether abroad or at home. We are called to be the hands and feet of Christ. We are His army, and we have Earth to conquer. God has commissioned us to be His soldiers. There is nothing to fear.

Week 11 Remain Steadfast

Crossroads

*For you have been my refuge, a strong tower against the enemy.
Psalm 61:3*

During the past weeks, we have reoriented the picture of who we are in Christ. The process revealed that all Christians must focus on the Lord's business. Week eleven focused on encouraging us to stand firmly in Christ as we launch into ministry. When we step away from our learnings, the devil will take us back to square one. As a called warrior of God, stepping away is not an option. We must remain steadfast, and this includes reaching out to others and leaning on one another. Remember, there is strength in numbers we cannot survive alone.

And let us not grow weary of doing good, for in due season we will reap, if we do not give up. Galatians 6:9

Week 12 Reaching Further

Crossroads

For I am not ashamed of the gospel, for it is the power of God for salvation to everyone who believes, to the Jew first and also to the Greek. Romans 1:16

One could experience YOUR4 anywhere in the world. Regardless, mission starts at our front door, wherever that may be geographically and whatever its composition. We are always on mission. We will not find a disciple of Christ who believes location affects mission. We are on mission every day. Christ did not start and stop during his mission, and neither will true disciples as they follow Christ's lead. As front doors change, mission stays the same. We are to "Go."

One of my favorite Psalms is 139. Psalm 139 tells us where we can minister. It tells us that Christ is everywhere. Knowing Christ is with me assures me that I can minister everyplace the sole of my foot touches. I can glorify God in my daily goings at home or abroad.

> *Where shall I go from your Spirit? Or where shall I flee from your presence? 8 If I ascend to heaven, you are there! If I make my bed in Sheol, you are there! 9 If I take the wings of the morning and dwell in the uttermost parts of the sea, 10 Even there your hand shall lead me, and your right hand shall hold me. Psalm 139:7-10*

YOUR4 Hiking and Climbing provided us with the tools we need to be on mission daily.

9 DAILY LIFE

28" Come unto me, all ye that labour and are heavy laden, and I will give you rest. 29 Take my yoke upon you and learn of me; for I am meek and lowly in heart: and ye shall find rest unto your souls. 30 For my yoke is easy, and my burden is light." (Matthew 11:28-30)

The three verses above cannot be held tightly enough to the Christian heart. The words convey a promise made and a promise kept regarding redemption. The words so eloquently and personally describe the depth of God's love. Three simple verses teach us why we should be compassionate as followers of Christ as we shine a light on friends, loved ones, and strangers.

28" Come unto me." Jesus calls us to himself. He does not call us to a second in command or to an angel. He calls us to Himself. We have been called to the King of Kings. He calls us personally, which speaks to our importance in Christ's eyes.

If Jesus is calling us to Himself, to whom are we calling people? Woe to any man that would call people to himself. We are to point all mankind to Christ. We do this through our display of love for one another and those around us. Not one person is exempt from our love.

Our calling to love others is also a summons to join the body of Christ. Speaking into each one's life with love and compassion draws us together. We are to love each other and those around us by learning more about God's love for us. No man is capable of loving others without Christ's direction. His calling and our obedience to the call demands we follow the footsteps that Christ so eloquently displayed during His earthly ministry.

Charles Spurgeon speaks of this calling as follows:

> *"'Come,' he drives none away; he calls them to himself. His favorite word is 'Come.' Not, go to Moses – 'Come unto me.' To Jesus himself, we must come, by a personal trust. Not to doctrine, ordinance, nor ministry are we to come first, but to the personal Saviour." (Spurgeon)*

To Jesus we must come before we will submit to Go!

" All ye that labour and are heavy laden."

Christ's call to those burdened is an offer of relief to those who realize self-sufficiency leads to destruction. Most of the time, God's path calls us to do more than we believe ourselves capable, but He is always next to us as we traverse each step.

We tend to go through life, placing laborious tasks upon ourselves seeking satisfaction or completeness. Christ calls us to Him to experience what we lack in satisfaction and completeness.

YOUR4 Hiking sought to build the foundation for reaching further for the gospel. We acquired a clear understanding of salvation and its effects on daily life. This groundwork was laid in the first seven weeks. We evaluated and learned to break down barriers that veiled our spiritual eyes and prevented us from answering our call. The burdens of religious rituals without Christ prevents us from growing, serving, and leading. We must not buy into ritualistic activities that hinder true worship. We cannot allow man to place religious burdens on our shoulders as these yokes are heavy and painful. Searching God's Word and learning to put His yoke upon us will be delightful. His path requires humility, and there we find strength in weakness, hope in hopelessness, and peace in turbulent times.

We quickly moved to Hike Mt. Trivergence. There we learned to deepen our learning and to bring others into our circle of influence and relational ministry. The further we traveled, the more we understood why we must enter through the narrow gate spoken of earlier. Entering by the narrow gate requires us to squeeze every life decision through this gate. This sounds simple. Once we know the size of the gate, we bring items through with us that will fit. Yet we quickly realize that as we draw closer to God, our gates shrink. The gate narrowing always reveals our more authentic selves and calls for us to let go of something to reach further for the Kingdom. We must shrink to self just as the gate to Christ shrinks, and as we grow in Christ. The more we dig into who we are and what our hearts contain, the more we realize how narrow this gate must become to remove our sin.

10 THE BODY

How do we view the church? Is this a group that does things differently than another body and considers it the only way? We cannot determine the nature of a church based on man's thoughts unless we are grounded in the Word. Today, I hear of missional communities, relational ministries, mega-churches, or community churches. Within all of this, we have decided there is a competition because one has more people. The body of Christ is not a competitive organization. Approaching worship differently does not or should not separate the body of Christ. If all worship points to God with Jesus as Savior, then we are all part of the Body and should worship, evangelize, and outreach as one.

Small groups are not only called to the people in our living room each week but also to those around us and the body of Christ. Large gatherings, please know that small groups worshipping Christ in a missional community versus large corporate meetings are not enemies. All factions of Christ's body must realize that we are called to witness to people in multiple ways. The missional community may be the only way to reach some while corporate gatherings reach others. Whatever the case, we fight the same battle. Therefore, we must come alongside each other and set our sights on the enemy rather than attacking each other. Look for ways to become part of the local church in support of their missions. Large gatherings start questioning ways to support the small group down the road and encourage them to reach further. As we learn to be the family God has called us to be, the world will desire to know more about us. Isn't that our goal? Reaching further will not be accomplished by one group, whether sitting in a building or a jungle hut. Our reach expands by the collective work of the glorious body of Christ.

CONTACT YOUR4 MINISTRIES

YOUR4 Ministries is available to walk with pastors through the discipleship method. We also support your gatherings through preaching, teaching, or evangelistic engagements. Christ has called us to be one body in Christ.

We would love to share in your list of keywords from the daily S.O.A.P.S. Share your hiking journey through Mount Convergence and Mount Trivergence, allowing us to rejoice within the body of Christ through your accomplishments.

Connect with us online at:

www.YOUR4.net

Email: brettbodiford@hotmail.com

Subject: YOUR4 Discipleship

YOUR4 Ministries is available for engagements such as: Preaching, Conferences, Church Leadership consults regarding YOUR4 Discipleship.

Made in the USA
Columbia, SC
10 September 2020

20199203R00152